Here it is. The story behind Patrick Henry's famous "Give me liberty or give me death!" speech – the motive behind Dunmore's many provocations, the revelation of Dunmore's and Henry's shared desire "to bring on a war as soon as possible" and a long-overdue account of the tragedy that powered the speech.

The *bête noir* in Dunmore's war against Virginia was always Patrick Henry, who, when he was not responding to one of his Lordship's outrages was devising one of his own. John Page, a Council member who knew them both, would later say that Patrick Henry "did actually bully [Lord Dunmore]," adding that "they appeared to me to be mutually afraid of each other." Was it fear of Henry that caused the Governor to abandon the palace in the middle of the night? Was it respect for the Crown that caused Henry to suspend his march on Williamsburg? Whatever the case, the private war between Lord Dunmore and Patrick Henry would go a long way toward deciding the course of the revolution in Virginia.

PRAISE FOR OTHER BOOKS IN THIS SERIES

"I LOVE these books . . . these are journeys of discovery, disclosing crucial new ways to read the motivations of very complex characters. Morrow gives me all I need to be judge and jury both. It's his engagement with people that I so admire: real, flesh and blood people – the flippant Rev. Camm, the irascible Gov. Fauquier, and the ultimately rather sad story of Arthur Lee and James Mercer. So very few historians have that skill. For them, the people remain documents on the page, and History, not life, claims them."

COLLEEN ISAAC

GEORGE T. MORROW II

"We Must Fight!"

The Private War Between
Patrick Henry and Lord Dunmore

WILLIAMSBURG IN CHARACTER

"We Must Fight!"
The Private War Between Patrick Henry and Lord Dunmore

Published by Telford Publications*

Design by Andrew Evans Design
Cover illustration by David Eccles

© George T. Morrow II 2012

Telford Publications
301 Mill Stream Way,
Williamsburg, VA, U.S.A., 23185

Tel (757) 565-7215
Fax (757) 565-7216
www.williamsburgincharacter.com

FIRST EDITION

**Telford Publications is named for Alexander Telford,*
a volunteer rifleman from Rockbridge County, Virginia, who
served in three Revolutionary War campaigns, in the last of which,
Yorktown, he was personally recognized by Gen. George Washington
for his extraordinary marksmanship with the long rifle.

Library of Congress Control Number: 2012938407
ISBN 978-0-9831468-6-5
Printed and bound by Sheridan Press, 450 Fame Avenue, Hanover, PA

"We Must Fight!"

The Private War Between
Patrick Henry and Lord Dunmore

George T. Morrow II

WILLIAMSBURG IN CHARACTER

Colonial Williamsburg's Patrick Henry (Richard Schumann) leads the
Hanover militia in a march on Williamsburg

"He spread before their eyes fields still floating with the blood of their
countrymen"

To Joan

"If a man could say nothing against a character but what he can prove, history could not be written."

SAMUEL JOHNSON

Contents

List of Illustrations

Errata

"We Must Fight!"

"We Must Fight!"

On April 21, 1774, a detachment of British marines, acting under orders from Gov. Dunmore of Virginia, seized 15 barrels of gunpowder from the Magazine in Williamsburg. Just three days before, the Military Governor of Massachusetts, Gen. Thomas Gage, had tried to arrest rebel leaders Samuel Adams and John Hancock and seize a cache of military supplies at Concord. This was not a coincidence. In a January 27, 1774 letter, Lord Dartmouth, Secretary of State for the Colonies, had ordered Gen. Gage to arrest "the principal actors . . . of the Provincial Congress"[1] – this on top of two earlier directives, issued to all of the royal governors, including Gov. Dunmore, to "take the most effectual measure for arresting, detaining, and securing any Gunpowder or any sort of Arms or Ammunition which may be attempted to be imported into the Province under your government."[2] So it happened that a precaution taken to avoid armed conflict ended up producing a revolution.

There were differences between the situations in Massachusetts and Virginia, however. Unlike the Virginians, who would remain peaceful until Lord Dunmore's late-night "elopement"* on June 8, 1775, the people of Boston had already experienced one "massacre" (March 5, 1770), a "tea party" (December 16, 1773)

---

* The term comes from a report issued by the Virginia House of Burgesses. Though now used mostly in connection with unmarried couples, it has always signified an unlawful act, as in the "elopement" of a thief.

and, as punishment for the latter, five parliamentary "Intolerable Acts," one of which provided for the quartering of British soldiers in the houses of Massachusetts citizens. To set against this litany of crime and punishment, Virginians had just one speech by Patrick Henry. But what a speech! Speaking on March 23, 1775 at St. John's Church in Richmond, Henry had described the prospect of war between England and America as a choice between liberty and death. On May 2, 1775, following another fiery speech to the county militia (The "Independent Company of Hanover"), Henry led a march on Williamsburg to recover the barrels of gunpowder "stolen" by Lord Dunmore. The arrival of a rider from Boston on April 28 with news of "the shot heard round the world,"* the Battle of Lexington and Concord, added urgency to what might otherwise have gone down as mere irritability. Most Virginians, George Washington included, had hoped that Patrick Henry would just take his men and go home. Fortunately, Henry could always count on Dunmore to supply him with an excuse, belated though it might be.

At first word of Henry's march, his Lordship had summoned the marines, armed his slaves and barricaded himself in his palace. Two cannons were secured from a British warship, the H.M.S. *Fowey*, to stand guard at the gate, while three Indian Chiefs, hostages to a recent peace agreement, patrolled the ramparts. There would be no battle. Having received payment in full for the seized gunpowder from the King's Receiver General, Richard Corbin, Henry and his militia reluctantly returned to Hanover. With war averted, Dunmore then thundered out a proclamation in the spirit of one of Henry's own addresses, sarcastically terming him "the said *Patrick Henry*" and calling on his "deluded followers" to desist.3 As Robert L. Scribner, the acerbic

---

* The line is from the poem, "Concord Hymn," written by Ralph Waldo Emerson for the city's Independence Day Celebration of July 4, 1837.

editor of *Revolutionary Virginia, the Road to Independence* put it,

> [H]ad his lordship taken employment as Henry's public-
> ity agent, he could not have raised his client to an
> eminence more lofty, and he may even have assured his
> enemy's election by the Third Virginia Convention as
> commander in chief of the colony's two-regiment 'army.'
>
> The scene in Virginia was now that of a drama the
> script of which was being written by the actors them-
> selves as they played their respective roles. Each actor
> was a free agent, except as he was molded by his consti-
> tutional ideology and his personal limitations. But
> consistency is, after all, a requisite of characterization.[4]

As Scribner viewed it, Virginia's Revolution was less the result
of events than of personalities; less the product of a misunder-
standing than of a mutual conviction that "After all, we must
fight."[5] Those were Henry's words, and when they are com-
pared to Dunmore's December 24 reply to the King's rebuke,
"these Virginians should be made to suffer the misery of which
they themselves are the author," it is clear that Henry and
Dunmore were of one mind about the inevitability of war.[6] Had
it not taken weeks for the Governor's letters to reach London,
he might have been stopped. Had Henry not been an oratorical force of nature, Virginians might have given peace a
chance. But both men were effectively beyond recall, and what
they achieved together, revolution and war, though it would
later be ascribed to political differences, was actually the result
of irreconcilable similarities in character aggravated by contempt on one side and a bottomless need for revenge on the
other.

I have spoken before in these pages of slavery's effect on the
character of Virginians, citing, in this connection, an observation
by the 18th Century English traveler, Andrew Burnaby: "Their

authority over their slaves renders them vain and imperious . . . The public . . . character of the Virginians corresponds with their private one: they are haughty and jealous of their liberties, impatient of restraint, and can scarcely bear the thought of being controlled by any superior power. Many of them consider the colonies as independent states, not connected with Great Britain, otherwise than by having the same common kind, and being bound to her by natural affection."[7] Slavery cannot by itself qualify as an all-purpose explanation for the political character of the Virginians, but it may help to explain the extreme irritability of the planter class on any matter affecting their liberties. Such a people might be flattered by a Botetourt, whose dignity and elegance of address could have charmed an entire army of Patrick Henrys, but they could never be ruled by a Lord Dunmore. Here is his Lordship's character, described as unfavorably as possible, by the anonymous "Virginius":

> To what fatality, my lord, can it be imputed that you, who had hitherto been considered as an inoffensive, easy, good-natured man, should suddenly become black as the Ethiop,* and prostitute abilities, never, indeed, designed to shine in the superior spheres of life, but which, in the calm retreats of social converse, if properly managed, exempt you from censure? . . . Does it necessarily follow, as an indispensable conclusion, because you have accepted an office from our most pious and gracious sovereign, that you must, Camelion like, alter your color, your complexion, your sentiments and, in short, that you must become the very reverse of what you were at the time of your investiture?[8]

---

* That is, an Ethiopian. A reference to Dunmore's plot to reduce Williamsburg to ashes by arming the slaves of patriots, but also an allusion to his Lordship's reliance on lies, schemes and chicanery – his "black arts."

It is the character of a fool and a Satan incarnate, a lapdog and a liar – in short, a complex man – and it has bedeviled the best efforts of historians to account for Virginia's revolution from the start, with one prominent Virginia rebel, Edmund Randolph, admitting that it was an uprising "without an immediate oppression, without a cause depending so much on hasty feeling as theoretic reasoning."[9] Randolph did not mean that Virginians had no grievances, only that revolutions are supposed to have causes, and the best he had been able to come up with was a vague feeling. To paraphrase Virginius, was this about British tyranny or how an easy-going governor became the reverse of what he seemed at his investiture?

Dunmore's only biographer, Percy Caley, summed up his character and career very well in 1934 when he wrote, "The present writer is constrained to record that, in his opinion, Dunmore, either in his private or his public character, was neither better nor worse than many another personage prominent in the annals of England and the United States . . . Had he received the unstinted support of the ministry and the British commander in America, and had he been provided with an adequate army and abundant funds, the loyalists of Virginia and the nearby colonies would have rallied to him in great numbers – and the historian, in all probability, would have had a different story to tell."[10] Dunmore's good friend George Washington, whose efforts to persuade the Governor to ignore his instructions and make grants of land to himself and other veterans supplied the occasion for the King's rebuke, had no doubt as to the depth of his anger or desire for revenge. He called Dunmore "a monster" whose hatred was equal "to the total destruction of the colony."* Richard Henry Lee would later say that the Ministry could not have found a better man

---

* See p.65, *infra*.

to ruin its cause than Dunmore.[11] It was meant as a joke. But the caricature produced by the Virginians' efforts to invest a tactless man with evil intent was no joke, and at least one writer has concluded that "if other events had not intervened, [Dunmore] might well have been recalled for being *too partial to the Virginians.*"[12]

The Governor's *bête noir* in his war against Virginia was always Patrick Henry, who, when he was not responding to one of Dunmore's outrages was devising one of his own. John Page, a Council member who knew them both, would later say that Patrick Henry "did actually bully [Lord Dunmore]," adding "but they appeared to me to be mutually afraid of each other."[13] Was it fear of Henry that caused the Governor to abandon his office in the middle of the night? Was Henry's bullying of Dunmore based on personal dislike or simply a tactic to bring on a war? These questions, which have been around from the first telling of the story of Virginia's revolution, have yet to receive adequate answers.

One thing is certain. Dunmore and Henry always make for a good story, with the former perhaps enjoying an edge when it comes to frustrating our best efforts to reduce him to a cipher:

Proud and insensitive, hot-tempered and vengeful, he certainly was – traits not wholly unknown, by the way, to the southern aristocracy – but scarcely brutal, unless all military commanders in the exercise of what they deem their duty may be so described. . . The charge that he was weak and unstable is unjust and unwarranted. In less stormy times he would have been judged able and reasonably efficient. In the face of great odds, under great handicaps, he moved with energy and enterprise, mistakenly perhaps at times, as events were to prove; but if adequate aid had been given him, the story might have been different . . . In asserting Virginia's authority over the Forks of the Ohio, he was backed by all the prominent Virginians who believed that Pennsylvania, had she ever had any rights to the region, had allowed them to lapse . . . Still, even if he had yielded, compromised, and tempered his words and actions, it is extremely doubtful that he could have stayed the course of events. 'The Moving Finger' of destiny was writing, and it is probable that neither the 'Piety nor Wit' of Dunmore, nor of any other man, would have been able to 'lure it back to cancel half a line.' The revolutionary ferment had pervaded all colonies, thus making it impossible for any one governor, no matter how astute or clever, to halt its progress.[14]

The outcome of this contest, war, was inevitable; it was only the terms that had to be decided. In Virginia, where character mattered, Dunmore's lies spoke as loudly as Patrick Henry's oratory. Had Dunmore remained what he seemed at his investiture – good natured – it is possible, but not likely, that peace would have prevailed. An easy-going governor might have delayed a revolution begun in a hasty feeling but he could not have stopped it.

Patrick Henry Tries to Bring on a War; Lord Dunmore Elopes

On Saturday, December 3, 1774, Charlotte, Lady Dunmore, was safely delivered of a daughter at the Palace in Williamsburg. She was named "Virginia" in honor of the colony her father had hoped never to see. The next day, Gov. Dunmore returned from his eponymous war against the Shawnee. Immediately, the Mayor, Recorder, Alderman and Common Council assembled to congratulate him on his late addition and the conclusion of his "dangerous and fatiguing Service."[15] Claiming to be "moved by an Impulse of unfeigned Joy," the President and professors of William and Mary also offered congratulations. To the latter, his Lordship expressed his cordial thanks, pointedly adding that every Instance of their attention gave him "a great Degree of Satisfaction." To the former, he offered a formal acknowledgement and a rather oblique rebuke, the more ominous-sounding for seeming to come out of nowhere, "I doubt not that, as I have hitherto experienced the Marks of your Civility, you will continue in the same friendly Disposition towards me."[16] For the city officials, Dunmore's sudden change in tone was as perplexing as it was unsettling. The events of the past 12 months – the closing of Boston harbor, the dueling "pleas" and "strictures"* in the *Gazette*, the election of delegates to the First Continental

---

* For Robert Carter Nicholas' *Strictures* on Attorney General John Randolph's *Plea for Moderation*, see George T. Morrow, II, *Of Heretics, Traitors and True Believers* (Williamsburg, VA, 2011).

Congress and the decision of that Congress to impose a boycott – might justify some displeasure but hardly this barely-veiled threat. Was their affable, otherwise easy-going governor revealing unexpected complexities? Unsure of what to say, they said nothing – with the result that Dunmore may have distrusted them even more.

On January 19, 1775 the Governor hosted an elegant entertainment at the Palace to celebrate his daughter's christening and the Queen's birthday. A numerous company of ladies and gentlemen attended, including James Parker, a loyalist Scottish merchant from Norfolk, who described Dunmore as "popular as a Scotsman [could] be amongst a weak prejudiced people."[17] For all the tension in the air, everyone seemed to have a good time, despite some uneasiness about Dunmore's intentions and some muttering about his reluctance to issue writs for a new Assembly. Had his guests known what their genial host had in mind for them as revealed in his reply, written less than a month earlier, to a stern reprimand from Lord Dartmouth, Secretary of State for the Colonies, they might have felt a little less like dancing:

These undutiful people [Dunmore wrote] should be made to feel the distress and misery of which they have themselves laid the foundation, as soon as possible and before they can have time to find out ways and means of supplying themselves. Their own schemes should be turned against them, and they should not be permitted to procure underhand what they refuse to admit openly, and above all they should not be permitted to go to foreign ports to seek the things they want. Their ports should be blocked up and their communication cut off by water even with their neighboring colonies, and this could be done effectually with only one ship of force and a frigate and a couple of tenders. With this, and without any other force or expense, no vessel could stir out of the Bay of Chesapeake or approach any port of Virginia.[18]

Having effectively laid a curse on his own subjects, the Governor then went on to advise Dartmouth and the Board of Trade as to what should be done with his "now entirely obstructed" government:

> The functions of every department of government, which in fact are now entirely obstructed, should be suspended and the governor and all other officers withdrawn. The people, left to themselves and to the confusion that would immediately reign, would I cannot but believe soon become sensible from what source their former happiness flowed and prostrate themselves before the power which they had so lately considered as inimical and treated with contempt.[19]

Five and a half months later, in the middle of the night of June 8, 1775, Lord Dunmore took his own counsel, eloping with his family to the H.M.S. *Fowey*, now anchored in the York River. With the exception of his friend John Randolph, whose home his Lordship had visited the evening before his departure, Virginians were taken by surprise. For all the turmoil of the intervening five months – most of it the result of Dunmore's own actions – no one, not even his enemies, expected him to simply walk away. It was just three weeks later, that "Virginius" was moved to wonder in Pinckney's *Gazette* how someone of such "prostitute abilities" could "suddenly become as black as the Ethiop."[20] For Edmund Randolph, the governor's sudden change of heart was due to "substantial barbarism not palliated by a particle of native genius nor regulated by one ingredient of religion."[21] Perhaps the harshest criticism of all came form Dunmore's one-time friend, George Washington, who called him, simply, "a monster." Washington did have some reason to be upset: a rumor, reported by his cousin Lund Washington, that Dunmore intended to sail up to Mount Vernon, seize Martha Washington and hold her hostage. Washington did not fully believe the story, but he had no doubt of Dunmore's anger toward himself or Virginians in general, his Lordship being "actuated . . . to a degree equal to the total destruction of the Colony."[22]

In July of 1774, sitting at his dining room table with his beautiful and accomplished Lady by his side, Dunmore seemed to Augustine Prevost to be angry with no one, not even the Shawnees. Prevost, a British army recruiter who would later meet up with his Lordship at his war camp near Pittsburgh, described his demeanor that summer as that of "a jolly, good hearted companion."[23] Certainly one reason he was jolly was that war against the Shawnees gave him a chance to redeem himself in the eyes of Virginians, who had long complained of "grievous oppressions" by the government of Pennsylvania. Defending Virginia's boundaries was another. But for Dunmore personally, it was the allure of the lands of the Ohio, whose forks at Pittsburgh had been described to him and Washington as the gateway to the west in "an extensive & Political Sense."

The Governor had already made one trip to Pittsburgh in July of 1773, his host on that occasion being the notorious adventurer and former Indian agent Dr. John Connolly. A promise of 2,000 acres on the Ohio was all it took to convince Connolly that his Lordship was "a Gentleman of Benevolence & universal Charity . . . not unacquainted with men or the World."[24] Since then, Dr. Connolly had been arrested by Arthur

St. Clair, the magistrate of Pennsylvania's Westmoreland County, released on parole, raised a militia army, seized Fort Pitt (which he renamed "Fort Dunmore") and returned St. Clair's favor by arresting several Pennsylvania magistrates. Meanwhile, the usual atrocities had added an Indian war to a territorial feud between two colonies. Dunmore could truly say that his war against the Shawnees was undertaken at Virginians' request. But it is also true that unrest among the Indians was a reaction to Connolly and his settlers and that the Governor's primary motive in going west was to scout out lands for himself and his friends.

Lust for land and service to one's friends were core tenets of the Dunmorean ethos. As it happened, these were also the qualities that George Washington valued most in a governor. Certainly Washington had courted Dunmore relentlessly since his arrival in 1771, urging him to use his authority as governor of Virginia to make good on Lt. Gov. Robert Dinwiddie's 1754 proclamation awarding 200,000 acres of land to Virginia veterans of the French and Indian War. Dunmore was soon thinking of Washington as a friend and potential business partner who not only shared his interest in land but knew the Ohio area well enough to direct him to the choicest parcels. Washington had in fact intended to go with Dunmore to Pittsburgh in 1773 to scout the area. Sadly, the death of his stepdaughter Patcy intervened, and his Lordship ended up making the trip alone –though he did send a note to "condole with [Washington] & poor Mrs. Washington for your loss."[25] Washington may not have known that Dunmore had recently filed a request for a grant of 100,000 acres in the western regions of Virginia, but he probably would not have been surprised.[26] He was himself secretly buying up the claims of impoverished Virginia veterans through an intermediary. Meanwhile Washington continued to urge Dunmore to make grants of land on his own authority – this despite the fact that Dunmore had told him "he did not think he was impowered to do so."[27]

Lord Dunmore's war against the Shawnees turned out to be a success in all respects. While a separate battalion under the command of Lt. Col. Andrew Lewis, an able veteran of the French and Indian War, did most of the fighting, his Lordship busied himself with Mrs. Connolly, a "diabolical serpent," according to Augustine Prevost, but one "tossed off most prodigiously fine." Dunmore told Prevost that he thought "Indian matters would be easily accommodated, but that the other troubles . . .were not likely to be so soon adjusted" – meaning the trouble with Pennsylvania. From the start, his Lordship made it clear that he intended to conclude a peace with the Shawnees. This is not to say that he feared war; if anything, he seemed entirely insensitive to mortal danger. Prevost was shocked to come upon him one afternoon far from camp "alone with his fusee slung & his hound." Why Dunmore should be out hunting alone in Indian country, Prevost did not say. But he had no doubt of his Lordship's skill with a gun; nor, it seems, with his ability to hold his liquor: "I gave him 7 bumper toasts which he could not refuse," Prevost reported later. "After dinner, we rose up & went to fire at [a] mark with rifles & pistols. I lost one bottle to my L[or]d, occasioned by my arms having been too long loaded & my being a little more affected with my drinking than he was."[28]

Like other observers, Prevost found Dunmore to be "extremely facetious & free," a description fully in accord with accounts of his Lordship as he appeared on his arrival in New York: "Short, Strong built, well-shaped with a most frank and open Countenance, easy and affable in his manners, very temperate, and a great Lover of field Sports, indefatigable and constant in pursuit of them." Though he had been told that Prevost's father-in-law, George Crogan, had "slandered [his] private character . . . [and called him] a bankrupt," Dunmore forgave Crogan *at their first meeting* – an act of such unexpected generosity that Prevost felt obliged to add "superior sagacity & profound Knowledge" in the ways that "nature opens to the human heart" to his catalog of Dunmore's virtues. Still, Prevost did not know "what to make of [the Governor's] . . . measures, or of his conduct." His proclamation expressing an intention to subject Pittsburgh to the jurisdiction of the laws of Virginia not only cut off a whole county from Pennsylvania, it "set the whole country in a blaze." Dunmore, Prevost wrote, "pretends that he acts by sanction of Lord Dartmouth, Lord of Trade." But far more shocking to Prevost than Dunmore's little lies was his failure to do any planning. He was setting off on a 500-mile trip down the Ohio River with "little or no provision, only a few canoes . . . [a] very few bad men & those all inclined to quit him & return to their habitation – [and] no money." Prevost's portrait of his Lordship at Pittsburgh is that of a "trifling" governor and "unfit" general, but an effective peacemaker; a liar, but one who easily forgave his enemies; a candid man who gave no hint of a darker side – except perhaps when it came to exploiting the weaknesses of other men.[29] Yet, within five days of his return from Pittsburgh in December of 1774, Dunmore was already revealing uncharacteristic irritability and within three weeks, demanding that Virginians be punished. What had changed him from a jolly, inoffensive soul into someone who "seemed actually to want war" was to remain a mystery, not only to his enemies, but it would seem, to historians as well.[30]

Certainly, Lord Dartmouth did not expect his September 8, 1774 rebuke of Dunmore to light a fire under him so fierce that it would engulf all of Virginia. Nor was Dunmore the only Virginia governor to be sternly reprimanded for failing to follow his instructions. Francis Fauquier had been rebuked by

Lord Hillsborough for his "leniency" towards Virginians, but his reprimand, brutal though it may have seemed, never accused him of "gross indignit[ies] and dishonor to the Crown" nor of acts of "inhumanity and injustice to the Indians" – acts so outrageous that only His Majesty's "tenderness and lenity" had kept Dunmore from being immediately recalled from Virginia:

> I am . . . commanded by the King to signify to your Lordship His Majesty's just displeasure that such a proceeding as that to which your letter refers should have received any degree of countenance or encouragement from you, and it is not without real concern that I find myself obliged to observe to your lordship that if His Majesty had not been graciously pleased out of his great tenderness and lenity to suppose that your conduct upon this occasion has proceeded from inadvertency . . . it must have been followed by other marks of the royal displeasure.[31]

What had he done? Dunmore turned to the letter which evidently had given the King such offense. It was his letter of May 16, 1774, the one in which he had recommended the approval of a petition from some Virginians who had purchased a large tract of land from the Indians on the Ohio River. Knowing that he was expressly prohibited by his instructions from allowing settlements on these lands, he had concluded his letter with an assurance that he would "omit no means in [his] power of putting His Majesty's intentions . . . in [his] instructions in full execution" – a statement so at odds with his true feelings that it can only be explained by reference to his great powers of self-deception. Indeed, he would later claim that "it would be most for the advantage of His Majesty that the lands in this colony should be permitted to be granted [by me] on the same easy terms to the inhabitants which they formerly were, which would certainly have the good effect of increasing the [King's] quitrents."[32]

He looked again at Dartmouth's letter. The Secretary was prepared to concede – for the sake of argument – that "it would be advisable upon grounds of general policy to allow settlements under the authority of the government of Virginia," but found the point irrelevant. As Dartmouth saw it, the "faith of the Crown . . . was solemnly pledged" by treaty and under that treaty, the King had personally pledged his "sacred word" not to allow settlement on Indian lands. Dunmore had not only failed to obey the Board's instructions, he had "dishonoured" George III, a matter of no little importance to a king who, perhaps unique among British monarchs, truly seemed to care about his integrity.[33]

There was more. Dartmouth and the King had clearly seen through his references to "*his* government" permitting grants of land. It was the King's pleasure, wrote Dartmouth, that he, Dunmore, declare His Majesty's disapprobation of the Petitioners' purchase in a "most public and solemn manner," an act of public contrition that was intended to be a personal lesson to him. This was followed by an emphatic order to not "make any grant or consent to any possession . . . of lands . . . proposed to be granted to Mr. [Thomas] Walpole," nephew of former Prime Minister Sir Robert Walpole, whose pending petition for 2,400,000 acres west of the Alleghenies was designed to absorb the competing application of Virginia's Ohio Company.[34] Finally, he was ordered to comply with the Board's previous order requiring him to transmit "lists of all grants

Lord Dartmouth
"Dunmore had dishonored the King"

of land made and passed within the colony of Virginia" and "make a like return every six months" hereafter – as if he were a mere schoolboy who needed to be monitored for cheating! He was not surprised to find that the Privy Council had also denied his request for 100,000 acres.35

If fear of discovery operated in Dunmore like guilt, being actually found out produced paradoxical feelings of injustice, obstinacy and rage (though not always at his detector). That was true now. To be sure, he was genuinely shocked and mortified by Dartmouth's rebuke. But he had no doubt of his innocence; and as he had no doubt, his reply makes compelling reading. Of course, he failed to note that one of the aims of his Pittsburgh trip was to scout land for himself. Nor did he see any need to repeat what he had told the settlers: that he was acting under Lord Dartmouth's authority. His task now was to prove a negative; or, as he put it, to show he was not "*so* criminal" as he was painted:

> The perusal of [your letter] has filled me with concern but not less with astonishment. I have gone over my own letter to which your lordship alludes and can only conclude that some other reasons than any which arise from the complexion of my own representation of the affair in question induced your lordship and the other of His Majesty's servants to set the matter before the King in so criminal a light that nothing but His Majesty's tenderness and lenity have saved me from the whole effect of the royal displeasure, and that by far the greatest part of it should be inflicted upon me.36

Instead of taking his medicine like a good servant of the King, Dunmore stood on his integrity. "I do not perceive the misconduct neither do I discover the justice of the heavy rebuke," he said. On the contrary, he was sure "that some malicious insinuations have been spread and received by your lordship and other of His Majesty's servants to my prejudice."[37] What sort of insinuations? "Perhaps the matter relates to land, probably an opinion may be entertained of my having been governed in this and other proceedings of that nature by views of interest to myself." He was right. Insinuations had been made, not by Dartmouth or by various unnamed Virginians, but by the man Dunmore so sneeringly described in his letters as "the proprietary governor of Pennsylvania." He would not stoop to speculate as to the reasons for Gov. John Penn's malice toward him. But he would answer his own question: "I have not in any manner whatsoever made a grant of land to myself, to any person of my family or even to any friend or connection, or made a grant to any other person for my or their benefit, or been concerned in any scheme for obtaining of land anyhow since I came to this government." At least the first part was true: he had made no grants to himself. But he *had* made grants of 200,000 acres to French and Indian War veterans from a list supplied by his friend Washington, in the process signing patents for 20,000 acres to Washington and himself. Many of these grants were within the Walpole tract; all were in direct violation of his instructions. The claim that he was not personally concerned in schemes for obtaining land was an out and out lie.

Most of the rest of Dunmore's long letter (it runs 50 manuscript pages) is taken up with a "full and explicit answer to all the particulars" of the charges lodged by Lord Dartmouth, a *tour de force* of injured innocence in which Dunmore, no doubt with editorial help from Capt. Foy, his six-foot plus clerk, personal bodyguard and all-around dogsbody, sought to reveal his better self:[38] his stout refusal to avail himself of "a plea of inadvertency . . . put in his way" by Lord Dartmouth; his insistence on "depend[ing] on the integrity of my actions and the uprightness of my intentions." His final point was that "the fear of losing the pecuniary advantages which I derive from His Majesty's favour will not induce me to use any other means [than his upright intentions] to ward off the reserved punishment with which I am threatened." He was daring them to fire him. How George III reacted to this letter is unknown. But at least Lord Dartmouth seemed impressed. He read portions of it on the floor of the House of Lords – with the result that on April 22, 1775 Virginians were able to read a fair sample of his Lordship's malice toward them in Dixon and Hunter's *Virginia Gazette.*

Dunmore was not fired. For lack of an alternative, with the hour of crisis already upon them, their Lordships at the Board of Trade had really no choice but to stand by their man. In the meantime, Lord Dunmore wanted revenge – not on George III or Gov. John Penn, both of whom were effectively beyond his reach – but on the undutiful people he presumed to govern. The question is, *why?* And why did it have to be *war?* If it was true, as he told Dartmouth, that "every step . . . taken by these infatuated people must inevitably defeat its own purpose," why not just allow the Virginians' boycott to produce the inevitable "scarcity which will ruin thousands of families?" Why not let "the lower class of people . . . discover that they have been duped by the richer sort?" Why was he so determined that Virginians should "feel . . . distress and misery . . . *as soon as possible?*"[39]

The short answer is, he never liked Virginia. He had asked for (and had been given) New York, only to then be sent, over his strenuous protests, to a Virginia still grieving for Lord Botetourt. He might have said that he tried to make the best of a bad bargain, had he not arrived a year late and had he not sought to use the powers of his office to enrich himself and his friends. Typically, he did not see why the appointment of Capt.

Foy as Deputy Auditor General, a position formerly held by Council President John Blair Sr., should not be at his disposal instead of the Speaker who had previously exercised this power. Nor did he understand why increasing Capt. Foy's fees should be controversial. To his surprise, as he told Lord Hillsborough, Virginians "talked of the fees in the light of taxes."[40] "Fearing disturbances," he then asked the House to rule on the propriety of the fees *ex post facto*. Only after applauding Dunmore's "Wisdom and Goodness in embracing so early an Opportunity of expressing your Willingness, if [the fees] should be found disagreeable to us, as they really are, to have them totally abolished," did the House get around to saying "no."[41] But the point was made – and taken – that the Governor saw his office as a bundle of perks to be meted out to himself and his friends. The fact that he was following the long-established English practice that an office, once granted, became the property of the occupant, was never taken into account – unfairly, as it seemed to Dunmore.

Sometimes, he was wrong even when he did everything right. His issuance of a warrant ordering the sheriff of Pittsylvania County to arrest five forgers who had been plaguing the colony with a "masterly forgery," (portrayed by Treasurer Robert Carter Nicholas as a grave threat to Virginia's "prosperity & commerce,") was a particularly painful case in point.[42] This time, he had sought advice from the Treasurer, Speaker and Attorney General *before* he acted. All agreed that, as it would be "ineffectual" to examine the culprits in the county of their arrest as Virginia law required, they should be brought to the capital for interrogation and trial. Though the House commended Dunmore for his prompt action, it noted the irregularity of his procedure and "humbly entreated" him "to not in future be drawn into Consequence or Example." Dunmore's reaction to this rebuke was consistent with his lifelong hyper-sensitivity to criticism. But what it also revealed – at least to unbiased observers – was that he had some cause for complaint himself:

> I acted in this Affair with the greatest Caution, and took the advice and assistance of Gentlemen, in whose Judgement, Candour, and Integrity I could confide. . . I little imagined when I was endeavoring to punish the Guilty, that my Conduct could by any means be thought to endanger the safety of the Innocent. If I have done amiss the same method will not be repeated; but if it should be determined to be regular, I shall continue to exercise the Powers I am invested with, whensoever the exigencies of Government, and the good of the Country requires such exertion; and under such Circumstances, I am persuaded that no one (even the most timid) will be under the least Apprehension, that this proceeding may in future be drawn into Consequence or Example.

That he had acted solely for the good of the Country and that the three officers he had relied on for counsel had lacked the courage of their convictions was, to Lord Dunmore, as clear as clear could be. The fact that it was Patrick Henry who had raised the objection in the first place, and that the House's leaders had bowed to a "force of nature," was also noted by him. As Dunmore saw it, he was surrounded by weaklings and hypocrites.

Sometimes he was right on both policy and morality. In 1772, he literally begged Lord Hillsborough to persuade the King not to veto an Assembly bill raising the import duties on slaves, noting that the bill was meant to achieve the "total expulsion" of slaves from Virginia.[43] The fact that Spain would find it easy to raise an army of Virginia slaves determined "to reveng[e] themselves," thereby effecting a quick "conquest of this country" was another reason. But Hillsborough had no hope that the government would ever approve a law restricting a trade so profitable to British merchants. Neither did Dartmouth. Yet Dunmore persisted, correctly noting on March 20, 1774 that vetoing such laws only served to "renew . . . the uneasiness which [the Virginians] often express at finding . . . a set of self-interested merchants . . . listened to preferably to . . . the people of the Colony themselves."[44]

Clearly Dunmore never fully realized how he was viewed in Virginia. Perhaps he enjoyed playing the part of the light-hearted roué. But he could hardly have enjoyed playing the fool. It might be illogical to seek revenge for his ill-treatment on an entire people, but his reply to Dartmouth and the outrageous acts of his last weeks in office suggest that is about what he did. In insisting that Virginians should "prostrate themselves" before the power they had "treated with contempt" he was looking not only for the respect due his government, but for the kindness due a much-abused friend.[45]

Dunmore's easy-going nature concealed more than undue sensitivity to criticism. His fierce identification of himself with his office is odd, even in an age addicted to prerogative. He was not merely reverting to the self-centered child when he fulminated about undutiful people. Though a Scotsman and a nominal Whig, Lord Dunmore adhered to Dr. Samuel Johnson's view that the dependencies produced by subordination were "conducive to the happiness of society."[46] But where Dunmore differed from Dr. Johnson was in his failure to display the dignity expected of someone in his station.[47] In fact Dunmore was in a special category among Scotsmen: he was the son of a Jacobite, one of those supporting the claims of Charles Edward Stuart, Bonny Prince Charlie, to the English throne. His father, the 3rd Earl, had offered to "come out" for the Prince in the 1745 rebellion, and it was only thanks to his brother, the 2nd Earl, a supporter of George II, that he was pardoned. This family background must have weighed heavily on the son, making him vulnerable to criticism and so determined to demonstrate his loyalty by his rough treatment of the insubordinate Virginians. In addition to the respect due an Earl and a Governor, Dunmore required attention to his needs. Ingratitude was not only a sin to him but a personal betrayal entitling him to revenge. Had he not always (to quote himself) tried to "labour toward . . . anything" that might help extend Virginia's "Commerce, open new Sources of Wealth and add fresh Motives, of mutual Benefit?" Had he not tried "to increase the dependence of [Virginia] and the Parent Country on each other?"[48] True, he had never failed to think of the benefit to himself, but was not reciprocal happiness the whole point of government?

After his return from the north he began to feel that he was surrounded by ingrates and traitors, many of them supposed friends, whose interests he had labored tirelessly to promote. Among the latter was Treasurer Robert Carter Nicholas, whom Dunmore had once described as a person of great integrity. In his December 24, 1774 letter to Dartmouth, he seemed to take Nicholas' defection to the patriotic cause personally, citing his "disposition to constantly oppose government."[49] John Page Jr., was another disappointment, "a young Gentleman of singular good parts," whom Dunmore had had appointed to the William and Mary Board of Visitors only to find him opposed to the appointment of Dunmore's friend John Randolph to the same Board on moral grounds! But perhaps the greatest betrayal of all was that of George Washington, the would-be business partner and friend, whose obsession with land matched his own and whose insistence that he give effect to Lt. Gov. Dinwiddie's 1754 Proclamation had provided the occasion for the King's rebuke. The great shock awaiting Dunmore on his return from the west was that Washington was now counted among the leaders of the Whig opposition.

It is not hard to see why Dunmore wished to inflict the miseries of war on the Virginians. Among its other gratifications, war offered punishment for ingratitude and a reply to insolence. Nor were Lord Dunmore's views all that unique in a government used to thinking of itself as an indulgent parent vexed beyond endurance by a willful, ungrateful child (America). Dunmore did not fear war; he feared that it would come too late when Virginians had "means of supplying themselves." He did not want to avoid a conflict; he wanted to bring one on "as soon as possible."[50]

Dunmore was not the only one trying to bring war to Virginia in the spring of 1775. At the time of his Lordship's April 22 raid on the Williamsburg Powder Magazine, his first act of aggression as a model of British tyranny, Patrick Henry was heard to tell friends that it was "most fortunate," as it "would rouse the people from north to south to revolt."[51] He continued, "You may in vain talk to [the Virginians] about the duties on tea . . . these things will not affect them. They depend on principles too abstracted for their apprehension and feeling. But tell them of the robbery of the magazine, and that the next step will be to disarm them, you bring the subject home to their bosoms, and they will be ready to fly to arms to defend themselves." Ironically echoing Dunmore's advice on how to deal with the people of Virginia, Henry continued, "*that blow* which must be struck sooner or later, *should be struck at once* before an overwhelming force should enter the colony; that that habitual deference . . . [felt by] people toward the governor . . . should be dissolved and dissipated; that the revolution should be set in motion in the colony."(Italics in original.)[52] Great Britain "*will* drive us to extremities," Henry wrote another friend. "No accommodation *will* take place – hostilities will *soon* commence – and a desperate and bloody touch it will be."[53] Both Dunmore and Henry claimed to divine the future; both by May of 1775 thought that war was inevitable.

It had been ten years since Patrick Henry had uttered his treason on the Stamp Act. He was still the Assembly's best orator; still the fastest-rising, most popular lawyer in Virginia. He was also, following his 1773 acquisition of the Treasurer's law practice, one of its richest. That he should think of acquiring a home suitable for a man of his wealth and status was only natural. The property he chose was one of Hanover County's grandest, "Scotchtown," built in 1755 by soon-to-be disgraced Speaker John Robinson. At Robinson's death, it was bought by Council Member John Chiswell who in 1766 committed suicide after being charged with murdering his friend Robert Routledge. Five years later, Henry bought Scotchtown from Chiswell's estate. With its fine English basement, elegant dining room and central hall and secluded park-like setting, Scotchtown was and is (it was restored in 1949) the very type of a Virginia gentleman's house.[54] Sadly, misfortune continued to haunt it. Within days of her arrival, and only months after the birth of her sixth child, Henry's wife, "Sallie," became so insane that she had to be put in a "strait-dress" and locked in the basement. There she would spend the last five years of her life, cared for (and guarded) by a slave.

Sallie's illness was treated by the Henry family as a dark secret not to be disclosed even to friends. Only in 1810 did the son of the Henry family physician finally disclose the true nature of her illness:

Here [at Scotchtown] resided the most illustrious patriot and statesman at the breaking out of the American Revolution. Here his family resided, whilst Henry had to encounter many mental and personal afflictions known only by his family physician. Whilst his towering and masterly spirit was rousing a nation to arms, his soul was bowed down and bleeding under the heaviest sorrows and personal distresses. His beloved companion had lost her reason, and could only be restrained from self-destruction by a strait-dress. I cannot reflect on my venerable father's rehearsal of the particulars without feeling myself almost a bleeding heart.[55]

Modern visitors to Scotchtown are made aware of the intimacy of Henry's ordeal. The room in which Sallie was kept is under the main living areas of the house. The odd shriek or thud as Sallie moved restlessly about in the room below thus would have been audible to the entire Henry household.

It is unclear whether Sallie was violent, but that may not have mattered. She had to be confined, and putting her in the Williamsburg asylum was out of the question.[56] In those years (and for long afterwards), mental illness was viewed as a disgrace for the entire family – a disgrace which Patrick Henry as a rising lawyer might have felt that he needed to keep hidden. Still, in keeping it a secret, he was choosing to live with it as an omnipresent fact – as a resident of Scotchtown, and as a caring and loving husband who must have longed for an end to his *own* ordeal. Instead of being a restful retreat like the one described in the motto on another 18th Century house, "Traveler, the peace of mind you seek is here," Scotchtown was a prison for Sallie and all of its residents.[57]

Sallie died in February of 1775. On March 23, Henry gave the greatest speech of his life to the Second Virginia Convention assembled at a safe distance from Lord Dunmore in St. John's Church in Richmond. William Wirt's mostly fictitious account of Henry's "Give me liberty or give me death!" speech suffers as usual from its author's need to gild the oratorical lily. Even so, it is the essential point of departure for anyone who wonders how a mere speech could have started a revolution:[58]

'. . . *There is no longer any room for hope.* If we wish to be free – if we mean to preserve inviolate those inestimable privileges for which we have been so long contending – if we mean not basely to abandon the noble struggle in which we have been so long engaged, and which we have pledged ourselves never to abandon, until the glorious object of our contest all be obtained! We must fight! I repeat it, Sir, we must fight!!! An appeal to arms and to the God of hosts, is all that is left to us!

* * *

'The battle sir, is not to the strong alone; it is to the vigilant, the active, the brave. Besides sir, we have no election. If we were base enough to desire it, it is now too late to retire from the contest. There is no retreat but in submission and slavery! Our chains are forged. Their clanking may be heard on the plains of Boston! The war is inevitable – and let it come!! I repeat it sir, let it come!!!

'It is vain to extenuate the matter. Gentlemen may cry, peace, peace – but there is no peace. The war is actually begun! The next gale that sweeps from the north will bring to our ears the clash of resounding arms! Our brethren are already in the field! Why stand we here idle? What is it that gentlemen wish? What would they have? Is life so dear, or peace so sweet, as to be purchased at the price of chains and slavery! Forbid it, Almighty God! I know not what course others may take; but as for me,' cried he, with both his arms extended aloft, his brows knit, every feature marked with the resolute purpose of his soul, and his voice swelled to its boldest note of exclamation – 'give me liberty, or give me death!'[59]

Wirt did what he could with italics and exclamation marks to suggest Henry-esque crescendos. But the real *power* of the speech came from its fusillade of absolutes, its fierce sense of urgency. How much of this was Henry and how much Wirt or his sources is, as always, open to question. But the tone – that of a man driven to distraction and desperation – seems authentic. It was also noted by others: "Imagine [wrote St. George Tucker] that you heard a voice as from Heaven uttering [these] words as the doom of fate . . . and you may have some idea of the speaker, the assembly to whom he addressed himself and the auditory [i.e., audience] of which I was one." For Wirt, phrases like "doom of fate" were merely an invitation to evoke the supernatural orator. For Tucker, Henry's words were the "handwriting on the wall of Belshassar's Palace."[60]

Though the gestures Henry used to frame his words are often noted, they are seldom described in detail. That is too bad as the gestures are a gloss on the speech and a key to the speaker's state of mind. Wirt had little to say about what Henry *did* during his speech. Fortunately, Henry's friend Judge Roane was at St. John's that day and left a full account, albeit one recalled 30 years after the fact:

When he said, 'Is life so dear, or peace so sweet as to be purchased at the price of chains and slavery?' *he stood in the attitude of a condemned galley slave, loaded with fetters, awaiting his doom.* His form was bowed; his wrists were crossed;

his manacles were almost visible, as he stood like *an embodiment of helplessness and agony.* After a solemn pause, he raised his eyes and chained hands toward heaven, and prayed, in words and tones which thrilled every heart, 'Forbid it, Almighty God!' He then turned toward the timid loyalists of the House . . . and said, 'I know not what course others may take,' and he accompanied the words with his hands still crossed, while he seemed to be weighed down with additional chains. *The man appeared transformed into an oppressed, heart-broken, and hopeless felon.* After remaining in this posture . . . long enough to impress the imagination with the condition of the colony under the iron heel of military despotism, he arose proudly, and exclaimed, 'but as for me' – and the words hissed through his clenched teeth, while his body was thrown back, and every muscle and tendon was strained against the fetters which bound him, and with *his countenance distorted by agony and rage.* . . then the loud, clear, triumphant tones, 'give me liberty,' electrified the assembly. It was not a prayer, but a stern demand, which would submit to no refusal or delay . . . and, as each syllable of the word 'liberty' echoed through the building his fetters were shivered; his arms were hurled apart; and the links of his chains were scattered to the winds. When he spoke the word 'liberty,' with an emphasis never given it before, his hands were open and his arms elevated and extended; his countenance was radiant; he stood erect and defiant; while the sound of his voice and the sublimity of his attitude made him appear a magnificent incarnation of Freedom . . . and he closed the grand appeal with the solemn words 'or give me death!' which sounded with the awful cadence of a hero's dirge, fearless of death and victorious in death; and *he suited the action to the word by a blow upon his left breast with the right*

hand which seemed to drive the dagger to the patriot's heart
(Italics supplied).[61]

Common to all accounts of Henry's speech is the sense of its
great power *as a performance*. Yet if there is one thing we know
for certain, it is that it was received as absolutely authentic. It
was also, according to St. George Tucker, an eyewitness, pre-
ceded by an "animated debate."[62] Prominent among the
naysayers were Robert Carter Nicholas, Edmund Pendleton
and Richard Bland, with the Treasurer insisting that the militia
should be used only to "rectify errors," "not to alter or destroy
the Constitution." Yet, after Henry's speech the Treasurer was
so carried away he forgot all about the militia and called instead
for the recruitment of 10,000 regulars "for a war." He got off
easy: an elderly Baptist preacher listening at a window became
"sick with excitement," while Edward Carrington, son of
Henry's friend Paul Carrington, asked to "be buried on this
spot." Even Thomas Nelson Jr., an avowed moderate prior to
the speech, was said to have "convulsed" his friends by calling
on God to witness his resolve to repel the British "at the
water's edge."[63]

The final vote on Henry's war resolution is said to have been
sixty-five to sixty.[64] Following standard Parliamentary practice,
convention Moderator Peyton Randolph appointed Patrick
Henry (as mover of the resolution) Chairman of the Committee
for Virginia's Defense. Richard Henry Lee, who had seconded
the motion, was named the Committee's Vice Chairman. Other
members of the Committee included Thomas Jefferson,
George Washington, Dunmore's War veterans Andrew Lewis
and William Christian, the latter Patrick Henry's brother-in-law.
The moderates were represented by Benjamin Harrison,
Edmund Pendleton[65] and Robert Carter Nicholas.

Henry's portrayal of a slave transformed into a magnificent

incarnation of freedom left the faces of his audience "pale and their eyes glaring," looking (we are told) "beside themselves."[66] Had they known about the mad woman in the basement of Scotchtown, the spectacle of her over-wrought keeper bursting his chains less than two months after her death they might not have been so enthralled. Then there was the matter of Henry's odd ambivalence. Was this the hero's return or the hero's dirge? Was Henry hopeless, triumphant in death or just confused? In the end, it probably did not matter. War against the world's most powerful army was a daunting prospect in any case, and if brandishing a letter opener (as Henry was said to do in one account) helped to brace the mind, perhaps that was good enough.[67] Exhilaration, relief, guilt – all played some part in powering Henry's eloquence that day. For loyalist James Parker, it was Henry's "infamous insolence" that was most memorable: "he called the K[ing] a Tyrant [Parker told Charles Steuart], a fool a puppet & tool to the ministry Said there was now no Englishmen, no Scots, no Britons, but a Set of Wretches Sunk in luxury."[68] For devotees of irony, the sight of a slave owner enacting the slave triumphant may have endured the longest.

The Second Virginia Convention ended on March 27, 1775. On April 1, Dixon and Hunter published a summary of the convention's acts and resolutions, including Henry's call for "a well regulated militia."[69] They also printed the names of delegates chosen for the Second Congress, juxtaposed for ironic effect to Dunmore's proclamation asking "Magistrates and other officers to use their utmost endeavours to *prevent any such appointment of deputies.*" There may have been irony too in the fact that the Governor's successful war against the Shawnees had removed the one threat that might have kept back country radicals from attending the Convention. The fact that delegates offered thanks to "our *worthy* Governor . . . for his truly noble, wise, and spirited conduct on the late expedition against our Indian enemy" was surely of little consolation to him since, as Edmund Randolph later said, it was viewed by many as "an unfelt eulogium" "polluting" the Assembly.[70] In the end, his Lordship was left to stand helplessly by as the House, on the slim authority of the colony's 1738 Militia Act, ordered each county to raise and equip 30-man troops of horse and 68-man units of militia – an order that not only bypassed him as governor, but preempted the veto power of the King.

In a June 25 letter, Dunmore reminded Lord Dartmouth of his previously-expressed "expectation" that his proclamation would have no other effect than "exciting the further insults of the Enemies of Government here, in their free Animadversions upon Administration, and giving them occasion to urge, to the People, a Stronger Necessity of Continuing their unwarrantable Practices."[71] He did not bother to provide specifics. As he said, he had expected insults. But it is also true that he now welcomed them as a justification for war. Patrick Henry's speech might be (as one writer has put it) his "individual declaration of war."[72] But it was not Virginia's. In fact, most delegates thought they had voted for self-defense, not war. Aside from a few extremists, the soul most likely to take heart from Henry's speech was Lord Dunmore.

In fact, Henry's desperate tone – his expressed wish to bring on a war as quickly as possible – agreed very well with Dunmore's agenda for restoring his reputation with the King. The orator's insolence was also fortunate: it made the Governor's case for war that much stronger. All that he lacked was authorization from London. But had he not advised the firmest measures? And if he had advised Dartmouth was that not – under the rule of Dunmore – tantamount to permission? There was another reason he needed to act, a reason that even today is seldom acknowledged. The first of Dartmouth's two general instructions to all royal governors (received by Dunmore in March) *ordered* him, albeit as a precaution, to seize all stores of gunpowder within his jurisdiction. It thus turns out that Lord Dunmore's seizure of gunpowder from the Magazine in Williamsburg – the act which is most often cited as the cause of the revolution in Virginia – was literally his duty. Dunmore was not one to be deterred by scholastic distinctions between orders general and specific. Nor was he, since his rebuke, concerned about provoking the Virginians whom he had described to his council as "a head strong and designing people."[73] His concern, rather, was not to be accused of inaction.[74]

Unfortunately, it was done like everything else he did in Virginia: slyly but ineptly, and under a full moon, which meant that the theft was discovered before all of the gunpowder was removed. He then made things worse by lying about it; in conversation, and in a proclamation in the *Gazette*. This is not to say that his act lacked for forethought. Only the week before, Dunmore had procured a large wagon and the keys to the Magazine from its keeper, John Frederick Miller. Then, on the night of April 15, he had Capt. Henry Collins and fifteen marines from H.M.S. *Magdalen*, a British man-of-war anchored on the James River, secretly bring the wagon up to Williamsburg. For five long days, Collins and his marines remained hidden in the shrubbery behind the Palace. Finally, between three and four on the morning of April 21, they drove the wagon up to the gate of the Magazine and began, very quietly, to load the barrels of gunpowder. The upshot was described by Dunmore in a May 1 letter to Dartmouth: "tho' it was intended to have been done privately, Mr. Collins and his party were observed, and notice was given immediately to the Inhabitants of this place. Drums were sent through the

City. The Independent Company got under Arms."[75]

The Independent Company, Williamsburg's militia, mustered at the courthouse. Made up of students, apprentices and a few gentlemen, the company's most notable member was George Wythe, the 49-year-old Clerk of the House of Burgesses. Except for being equipped with a fowling piece, Wythe was attired like the other members of the militia; that is, "in the habit of the new American troops, wearing a shirt of coarse linen or canvas over their clothes and a tomahawk by their sides."[76] Less intrepid (and more circumspect) were the Speaker, Treasurer, Mayor and Common Council, all of whom tried to persuade the crowd, estimated at 1,500, not to try to retake the gunpowder by force.[77]

Dunmore's own version of the "commotion" (as a House committee later called it) suffered a little from his need to exaggerate the threat to himself, but it was otherwise accurate: "continued threats [he told Dartmouth in his May 1 letter] were brought to my house that it was their resolution to seize upon, or massacre me, and every person found giving me assistance, if I refused to deliver the powder immediately into their custody." Eventually, Mayor Dixon, with help from the

George Wythe
"Attired in the habit of the new American troops"

Treasurer and the Speaker, was able to persuade the mob to put its demands in a petition. The three officials then marched up the Green to the Palace as Dunmore watched from a window. He probably wished that he had Capt. Collins and his marines with him, but they and their wagonload of gunpowder were at that moment bouncing down a very bad country road to the James.

To his great surprise, his Lordship found the terms of the petition rather mild. The mob even accepted his rationale for seizing the powder: "various reports . . . that some wicked and designing persons have instilled the most diabolical notions into the minds of our Slaves, and that, therefore the utmost attention to our internal security is becoming the more necessary." Dunmore could hardly have asked for more. He told the delegation he would return the powder in "half an hour . . . on his word and honor" – should it be needed. That was enough for Dixon, Nicholas and Randolph, who made great use of his word of honor in dispersing the crowd.[78]

The next day, Dunmore reported to his Council on the events of the night before.[79] Unfortunately, his account belied what he had told the City officials – that he meant "to prevent the attempts of any enterprizing Negroes" – by candidly admitting that had he ordered the powder seized, "to anticipate the malevolent designs of the enemies of order and government." Warming to his task, Dunmore then told the Council that it was his "indispensable duty" to act. He was more specific in a Proclamation in the *Gazette*: "I think proper to declare that the apprehensions . . . of an intended insurrection of the slaves . . . and my knowledge of [the magazine] being a very insecure depository, were my inducements to that measure."[80] Having thus gone on record in Virginia as a serial obfuscator, if not a serial liar, he then told Dartmouth in a May 1 letter that his reply to Dixon *et al* was merely a "verbal" answer given in an "endeavor to soothe them." What he failed to add of course was that his proclamation was flatly contradicted by what he told the Council, and that at least one Councillor, self-described "Whig" John Page, had advised him to return the powder at once. He also failed to mention how he had greeted this suggestion: by flying "into an outrageous passion, smiting his fist on the table [and] crying, 'Mr. Page I am astonished at you.'"[81]

So many stories, so many lies. Had he thought about it, Dunmore might have taken comfort in the fact that he was not the first royal Governor to experience such difficulties. Yet, though he was obliged to do his duty for England, even to lie, Dunmore showed none of the anguish of a Fauquier and none of Botetourt's grace. [82] He not only lied about a slave insurrection, he admitted that he lied; and still not finished when he was done, took steps to turn his lies into actions.

It was now April 23, the second morning after the raid on the Magazine. According to a later report by the House "Committee on the Causes of the Late Disturbances and Commotions," the people of Williamsburg had "retired peaceably to their Habitations." Capt. Collins, his marines and Capt. Foy could be seen strolling about the streets of the city, unarmed and unmolested.[83] Later, they were joined by Capt. Montague and 40 sailors from H.M.S. *Fowey* (soon to be pressed into service as Dunmore's flagship). Dunmore would later tell Dartmouth that the crew of the *Fowey* just "happened to be in town."[84] Be that as it may, the city was quiet enough for Dunmore to send for a local physician, Dr. William Pasteur, to attend a patient whom Pasteur would later describe as a member of Dunmore's family. As he was leaving the Palace, Pasteur "accidentally" ran into the Governor, whom he found in a foul mood.[85]

According to Pasteur, Dunmore was still angry about the events of two days before. He "seemed greatly exasperated at the People having been under arms," Pasteur later testified. "[I told him] that it was done in a hurry and confusion; that most of the people were convinced they were wrong." His Lordship was not appeased. Instead, he "proceeded to make Use of several rash expressions and said that tho' he did not think himself in Danger yet he understood some injury or insult was intended to be offered to the Captains Foy and

Collins, which he should consider as done to himself as those Gentlemen acted entirely by his particular Directions." That Collins and Foy might suffer injury or insult was news to Pasteur, who had seen them strolling about town, and so he asked what these might be. It was something based on his Lordship's "understanding." But if Pasteur was confused by Dunmore's choice of words, his manner left him in no doubt whatsoever:

> His Lordship then swore by the living God that if a Grain of Powder was burnt at Captain Foy or Captain Collins, or if any Injury or insult was offered to himself, or either of them, that he would declare Freedom to the Slaves, and reduce the city of *Williamsburg* to Ashes. His Lordship then mentioned setting up the Royal Standard, but did not say that he would actually do it, but said he believed, if he did he should have a Majority of white People and all the Slaves on the side of Government, that he had once fought for the *Virginians*, and that, by GOD, he would let them see that he could fight against them, and that in a short time he could depopulate the whole Country.

Dunmore's threat packed all of the Virginians' worst nightmares into one ugly promise, featuring himself as Virginia's one-time friend, turned avenger for a crime visible only to himself. He would not thwart a slave uprising. He would lead one. He would not protect Williamsburg. He would reduce it to ashes; and, having done that, proceed to depopulate the entire colony. The fact that he had already commandeered four-fifths of the colony's supply of gunpowder, its primary defense against such insurrections, gave his threat credibility and terrifying urgency.

Pasteur was appalled. He apparently asked Dunmore if he meant what he said. The Governor took Pasteur's natural question as a dare. He told the doctor to "immediately . . . communicate this to the Speaker and other Gentlemen of the town, for that there was not an Hour to spare, adding also that if [militia leaders Alexander] *Finnie* and *George Nicholas* continued to go at large, what he had said, would, from some Misconduct of theirs, be carried into Execution."[86] With that, "the said Pasteur [as the House report put it] immediately communicated this matter to the Speaker and several other Gentlemen of the Town, and it soon became publicly known. In Consequence of which two of the principal gentlemen of the city sent their Wives and Children into the Country." The next day, again, Pasteur came upon Dunmore during a visit to the Palace. Again, he was told the "city would be reduced to ashes." This time the threat was quite specific: "if a large Body of People came below Ruffin's Ferry (a place thirty miles from the City) . . . he [Dunmore] would immediately enlarge his plan, and carry it into Execution, but [he added] . . . he should not regard a small number of Men, adding [that] he . . . had two hundred Muskets loaded in the Palace."

In the meantime, Pasteur had passed on Dunmore's threat to Benjamin Waller, Clerk of the Governor's Council, who felt such "great uneasiness" that when his Lordship stopped by his house a few days later on private business, Waller told him frankly that "he was very sorry to tell [him] . . . he had lost the Confidence of the People not so much for having taken . . . the Powder as for the declaration he made of raising and freeing the Slaves."[87] But Dunmore refused to be moved. "Yes," he declared, "he did say so and he made no secret of it." What is more, he told Waller, he "would do that or anything else to . . . defend . . . himself in case he [were to be] attacked," adding "that some slaves had offered him their services." This was, at the least, a gross exaggeration. Only a single slave had offered him his services and he was a member of Dunmore's own family. Still, there seemed to be no doubt that the Governor meant to carry through on his threat. A deposition taken a month later from John Randolph by Robert Carter Nicholas for the House "Committee on the Causes of the Late Disturbances and Commotions" indicated that though Mr. Attorney did "not recollect he heard the Governor expressly say he would proclaim Freedom to the Slaves . . . [he was] well satisfied that such was his Lordship's intention, if it had been necessary to take up Arms in defense of his Person."[88] In his final Report to the House, Nicholas tried to explain the impact of the Governor's threat. It was issued, he said, "when every Thing was perfectly quiet," "exceedingly alarming" people and causing them to think the raid on the magazine was part of a plan – an impression confirmed on April 24, the day after Pasteur's first conversation with Dunmore, when an express from Boston brought news that the Military Governor of Boston, Gen. Gage, "had sent an armed Force to seize a Provincial Magazine at Lexington."[89]

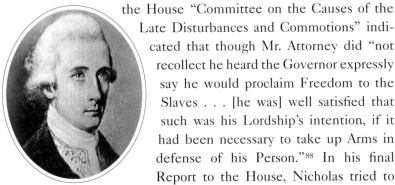

Benjamin Waller
"He felt great uneasiness"

As it happened, the news of the Battle of Lexington reached Virginia as the Fredericksburg Independent Company (militia) was gathering for its monthly training exercises. Immediately, the Company's Commander, Dr. Hugh Mercer, sent off riders to seek advice from the Speaker and Col. Washington, Mercer's commanding officer in the French and Indian War. Washington, whose diary for April 26 records a trip "up to Alexa[ndria] to meet the Ind[ependen]t Company," apparently advised Mercer against any sort of armed confrontation with his Lordship.[90] Meanwhile, Burgess Mann Page Jr. and the two other riders Mercer had sent to consult with the Speaker had met up with a rider on the same mission for the Independent Company of Hanover. Finding that the men of Hanover had also been put in a state of readiness and beginning perhaps to think of themselves as the vanguard of an insurrection, the five men elected to ride to the capital together.

We know little of their conversations there, except that Randolph, like Washington, advised restraint, and that his reason for doing so was Dunmore's promise to return the powder. That Patrick Henry, a member of the Hanover Company was now involved, must also have been in his thoughts. In any case, the Speaker wanted no part of a war. Unlike Washington, he put his warning against "violent measures" in writing, thus putting on record (in a lawyerlike way) his aversion to treason. Though he had agreed to take Washington's and the Speaker's counsel, Mercer could not resist sending off a note to Lord Dunmore vowing to resist tyranny "at the utmost hazard of our lives." He ended his note with a neat patriotic twist on the phrase his Lordship and other governors appended to their official proclamations – ("God Save the King!"): "God save the liberties of America!" [91]

As might be expected, the reaction in Hanover County was radically different. With a Patrick Henry to frame the issue, the Hanoverians were sure to conclude that a plot was afoot. As the Treasurer later put it, news of the Battle of Lexington so "increased the Apprehensions of our People, as it held out to them an additional Proof that the Steps . . . taken formed a Part of that general System adopted to render the Colonies

Peyton Randolph
"He advised restraint"

defenseless."⁹² Having been summoned to a meeting in New-castle, Virginia on what was termed "business of the highest importance to American liberty" and told to bring their mus-kets, the Hanover militia must have realized that revolution and war, not peace, was now the object and that if they were not under the command of Patrick Henry they were at least under his spell.⁹³

According to Wirt, Henry gave one of his best harangues in Newcastle. Stealing a leaf from Arthur Lee's *Monitor*s, he told the men that he suspected a plot to subjugate America. He then spread

> before their eyes, in colors of vivid description, the fields of Lexington and Concord, still floating with the blood of their countrymen, gloriously shed in the general cause; showed them that the recent plunder of the magazine in Williamsburg was . . . part of the general system of subju-gation; that the moment was now come in which they were called upon to decide, whether they chose to live free, and hand down the noble inheritance to their chil-dren, or to become hewers of woods, and drawers of water to those lordlings, who were themselves the tools of a cor-rupt and tyrannical ministry.⁹⁴

Lord Dunmore's raid on the Magazine was thus re-positioned as a chance to strike a "first blow" for liberty. As he often did, Henry drew upon the Bible for images of "wretched abase-ment" and "vassalage." Nor did he fail to note the parallels between Americans' struggle for liberty and that of the Jews. It was not long before "the meeting was in a flame and the deci-sion, immediately taken, was that the powder should be retrieved or counter-balanced by a reprisal." Company leader Capt. Samuel Meredith thereupon resigned in Henry's favor and the new Captain "took up his line of march for

Williamsburg."Other volunteers crowded to Henry's standard en route. 5,000 more were said to be on their way.[95] But Henry had misjudged Williamsburg's cooler heads. The same officials who had stood in front of the mob on April 22 to counsel patience now moved resolutely to stop him. The Speaker sent messenger after messenger, begging Henry to desist – only to discover that his riders had all been arrested and the newly-minted Captain was actually hastening his march on the capital.

By the 26th Henry was at Doncastle's Ordinary, sixteen miles from Williamsburg. There he made camp and held a council of war. Someone – perhaps even Capt. Henry himself – suggested that full payment for the gunpowder might be an acceptable alternative to bloody war. The suggestion was accepted, and a detail of sixteen men under the command of one Ens. Goodall was dispatched to "Lanesville," the planta-tion of the King's Receiver General, Richard Corbin. The idea was to hold Corbin and the King's "quitrents"* hostage for the value of the lost gunpowder. As it was still dark when he arrived, Goodall waited until morning before rousing the household. A polite knock on the door produced Mrs. Corbin – a woman born to be the equal of any army. No, Goodall was firmly told, Corbin was not at home. He was in Williamsburg, *with his quitrents*. What is more, Mr. Corbin and his quitrents were *always* at his office in the Capitol, *never* at home. "Would Goodall like to search?" A Virginia gentleman, Goodall pre-ferred to take a lady's word. He then apologized – twice – before excusing himself (war and Patrick Henry waiting for no man). It was as genteel an attempted kidnapping as could be imagined: a credit to Virginia, marred only by Ens. Goodall's

---

* Rents paid to the Crown by Virginia planters for the use of what was, still, the King's property

failure to re-examine his premises. Mrs. Corbin, it turned out, cordially hated her husband.

Goodall returned to find his chief conferring with Corbin's son-in-law, Carter Braxton, who had been at the Caroline County home of Edmund Pendleton when he heard about Henry's march. Braxton told Henry that if he attacked the Palace, Dunmore would raze the capital or Yorktown.[96] Would Henry be willing to let him see if he could persuade Mr. Corbin to pay for the gunpowder? Henry said that he would. Braxton then rode off to the capital where, after much talking by him and some help from Council President Thomas Nelson Sr., Corbin agreed to issue a check for £330 (the estimated value of the gunpowder) drawn on a Philadelphia bank. Braxton and Nelson then dashed back to Doncastle's to deliver the Receiver General's check and explain why they did not have cash.

A receipt in the Virginia archives tells the rest of the tale of the battle that wasn't.[97] Dated "Doncastle's Ordinary, New Kent, May 4, 1775," and in the handwriting of Capt. Henry himself, the receipt made two points of surpassing importance to its author: First, the powder was owned by Virginia and not the King. Second, it was Virginia's Assembly, not the British Parliament (and certainly not Lord Dunmore), who had the authority to determine its disposition. Henry had to be content with payment in full and an exploit that fell rather short of a revolution. He did write a wistful letter to Nicholas asking whether he needed an army to protect his treasury. The Treasurer was clear that he did not.[98] What is more, he doubted the propriety of such an army. Lord Dunmore did try to get in the last word. On May 6, he anathematized Patrick Henry as an outlaw.[99]

Whereas, I have been informed from undoubted authority,

that a *certain Patrick Henry*, of the county of Hanover, and a number of deluded followers, have taken up arms, chosen their officers, and styling themselves an Independent Company, have marched out of their county, encamped, and put themselves in a posture of war; and have written and dispatched letters to divers parts of the country, exciting the people to join in these outrageous and rebellious practices, to the great terror of his majesty's faithful subjects, and in open defiance of law and government; and have committed other acts of violence, particularly in extorting from his majesty's receiver-general the sum of three hundred and thirty pounds, under pretence of replacing the powder I thought proper to order removed from the magazine: whence it undeniably appears, that there is no longer the least security for the life or property of any man; wherefore I have thought proper with the advice of his majesty's council, and in his majesty's name, to issue this my proclamation, strictly charging all persons upon their allegiance, not to aid, abet, or give countenance to the said Patrick Henry, or any other persons concerned in such unwarrantable combinations; but, on the contrary, to oppose them and their designs by every means; which designs must otherwise inevitably involve the whole country in the most direful calamity, as they will call for the vengeance of offended majesty, and the insulted laws, to be exerted here to vindicate the constitutional authority of government.

On the same day, Dunmore sent his wife and family to the H.M.S. *Fowey* at Yorktown for safety, a decision John Randolph would later say was due to "the Timidity of [Lady Dunmore's] Sex."[100] He might better have attributed it to Dunmore, its true author, whose fears for his family's safety were at least equaled by his fear of inaction and his desire to bring on a war as soon as possible. If he had agreed to extortion it was because, for lack of an army of his own, he had little choice. Meanwhile, the said Henry was on his way to Philadelphia, "escorted in triumph by a large party of gentlemen." There he would join Washington, Jefferson and Randolph, already attending the Second Continental Congress, in crafting a Virginia-style resolution for the non-importation of British goods.[101]

If Virginia was not at war, it was not Dunmore's fault. As for Patrick Henry, his first biographer, Wirt, described him as "crowned with success," his men returning "in triumph."[102] The advice of the Speaker and Washington captured the sentiments of Virginia's soberer patriots. For conservatives like Braxton and Pendleton, Henry's exploit had raised the specter of a dictator. How loyalists felt was revealed by the garbled notice put in Rind's *Gazette* by William and Mary Prof. of Moral Philosophy Samuel Henley, who was so anxious for "ready money" to get home that he was willing to mark down a "Port Folio of NEGRAVINGS" (*sic*) by the "most celebrated Masters."* That he had some reason for haste was suggested by the notice immediately preceding his own: "A Serious ADMONITION" from an "anxious" "Civis" asking "Friends and Fellow Citizens" not to allow the "leaven of discontent" left over from Henry's march "to spread, and break out into fresh disorder."[103]

Dunmore's May 1 report on the affair, written while Henry and his rumored host of 5,000 was still en route to the capital, sug-

* For the story of Henley's many problems with the nabobs of Williamsburg, including his heresy trial, see George T. Morrow, II, *Of Heretics, Traitors and True Believers, the War for the Soul of Williamsburg* (Williamsburg, VA, 2011).

gested a man more in the grip of frustration than fear. He told Dartmouth that he meant to resist until he was driven from office. But he also made it clear that resistance was pointless. "I shall remain here [he wrote] until I am forced out. But as I cannot expect to be able to make any effectual resistance in this place against the number that are said to be moving towards me, I intend to retire towards the town of York where . . . under the protection of the guns of [the H.M.S. *Fowey*] . . . I shall . . .wait for His Majesty's orders." He added, as if by way of afterthought, "[I]t is my fixed purpose to arm all my own Negroes and receive all others that will come to me whom I shall declare free." Finally, he told Lord Dartmouth that he "consider[ed] the whole country in an actual state of rebellion and myself at liberty to annoy it by every possible means, and that I shall not hesitate at reducing their houses to ashes and spreading devastation wherever I can reach."[104]

What had seemed merely "several rash expressions" to Dr. Pasteur was now policy. Soon, policy would be fait accompli. The efforts of a Virginia Assembly hoping to diminish the British trade in slaves with higher import duties were to be superseded by the personal fiat of Virginia's British governor. *Dunmore* would free the slaves. *Dunmore* would put the country "in an actual state of rebellion." *Dunmore* would reduce Williamsburg to ashes and spread devastation throughout the country. And his authority for doing all this: the distance between London and Williamsburg; the practical inability of the King's ministers to say him "nay"; and the fears and furies of a man who viewed his office as an extension of himself.

On May 12, Lady Dunmore, to everyone's "great joy," returned to the palace. On May 20, the members of the Governor's Council published a notice in the *Gazette* assuring "the good PEOPLE of Virginia" they were not "a separate body of men" with interests "distinct . . . from the rest of their countrymen and fellow subjects" but "watchful guardians of the rights of the people." A few diehard Virginia loyalists may have believed that. But if a "gentle, mild and constitutional method" of redress were achievable, as the Council was insisting, why had it not spoken up before when it might have had some effect? [105]

It was now mid-May. With Henry in Philadelphia, his Lordship found himself, like Shakespeare's Cleopatra, sitting out that "great gap in time" while his rival was away. [106] Impatient, and growing more so by the moment, he still had not reduced Williamsburg to ashes. He decided to advance the cause of conflict and controversy by asking the city officials to join him in investigating the pilferage of muskets from the Magazine. In a later report to the House of Burgesses James Mercer described how the Magazine's keeper had incurred his Lordship's wrath by observing that the muskets left on the floor by looters had no firing mechanisms:

> The said John Frederick Miller [the keeper] and John Dixon, Esquire, Mayor of this city . . . were in the magazine (soon after the powder was said to be taken away) with his Excellency [Dunmore] who there mentioned that he had taken away fifteen barrels of powder; they then saw eight barrels, which they understood was powder; one being open . . . at the same time, they observed that the cleaned muskets were without locks; and the said Miller says his Excellency rebuked him for taking notice of that circumstance, and the said Dixon said he observed some persons had been in the magazine overnight, as he saw many arms lying in the yard of it; and his Excellency then told him, he had ordered the powder to be buried in the magazine yard, for though it was but dust, yet as he

understood some persons went in the magazine for arms in the night, with a light, they might set fire to the powder and injure the magazine.[107]

Not surprisingly, the Common Council condemned the thefts in the *Gazette* as an outrage. Equally unsurprisingly, their notice had little effect on the pilferers or their likely leader, James Innes, a recent graduate of William and Mary, whose oratorical skills were said to rival those of Patrick Henry. Impatient as always with the niceties of due process, the Governor then tried self-help, secretly ordering the mounting of two loaded shotguns opposite one of the Magazine's windows. Trip wires were attached to the triggers. When the thieves opened the window, the wires would trip, his "spring guns" would fire and the thieves would be instantly punished, judged and tried. The perverse efficiency of justice avenged before it was even done no doubt appealed to his Lordship.

His device worked, only too well. At 2 a.m. on June 3, three young men, one of them a William and Mary student, broke into the magazine. One of Dunmore's spring guns roared. The son of Mayor Dixon lost two fingers and two other men were wounded. Dixon's *Gazette* reported the incident on June 19, naming his Lordship as the "artful" author of the "horrid device." Purdie went even further, calling his Lordship a bad man, his spring gun a "diabolical invention." It is likely that both men, as well as most Virginians, were well acquainted with the controversial history of spring guns, a favorite device of the English squirearchy for dealing with poachers. As their victims were often the starving poor, these guns were both a source of outrage and a symbol of social injustice, against which even the precedent-bound English courts felt some compulsion to act. Dunmore could not have found a better way to destroy what was left of his frayed moral authority. This was no mere abuse of power. This was a crime against humanity by Virginia's first magistrate. In quoting Cicero on the tyrant Sulla (*"O tempora, O mores!"*) Purdie spoke for most Virginians.[108] Formerly the inept agent of an oppressive policy, Dunmore was now the very incarnation of British tyranny.[109]

News of his June 1 presentation to the Assembly of Lord North's long-awaited peace proposal (the "Olive Branch") was printed in both *Gazettes*, below or alongside more news of Dunmore's spring guns.[110] Whether or not the Olive Branch was (as William Pitt would later claim) "mere verbiage, a most puerile mockery" it was unquestionably America's – and Great Britain's – last chance for peace.[111] It deserved a fair hearing from a receptive audience. It also deserved a better advocate than a would-be murderer whose tortuous syntax belied his profession of sympathy for what he himself described as well-founded grievances:

> I have called you together [Dunmore told the House] to give you an opportunity of taking the alarming state of the colony into your consideration, and providing remedies against the evils which are increasing therein; and I am induced to it at this time particularly, because, as the declarations of the King and Parliament, contained in the joint address of the Lords and Commons on the 7th of February last, and his Majesty's answer, no longer admit of a doubt that your well-founded grievances, properly represented, will meet with that attention and regard which are so justly due to them.[112]

To be sure, Virginians were unlikely to agree to Parliament's request for the "gift" of a financial contribution "towards the public burdens of the [British] state," however it was styled.[113] Nor was it likely that they would meekly submit to Parliament's authority, the Olive Branch's true purpose.

In the style of his homilies to the House, the Governor ended his presentation with an exhortation: They should try to use "patience, calmness, and impartiality." By reflecting "upon the benefits this country hath received" from its "parent state," the burgesses could "convert our gloomy apprehensions into prospects of peace, happiness and lasting security." It was a fatuous remark. It was worse than that. To talk of "peace" with the smoke of his spring guns still hanging in the air was as despicable as his efforts to conciliate were half-hearted. He then told them that Parliament did not expect a prompt response to the offer. It was to be left open. But with the colony said to be in "an alarming state," that in itself must have seemed suspicious – which is to say his audience may have thought that Dunmore had not so much delivered an Olive Branch as abandoned it. He had not argued for peace. He had merely asked them to reflect on its prospects.[114] Four days later, on June 8, 1775, the reason for his diffidence became clear. In one final act of deceit he had eloped in the middle of the night from Williamsburg and set up a government in exile on the H.M.S. *Fowey* at Hampton. With him were Lady Charlotte and his children, John Randolph's wife and children and the adjudged heretic, Prof. of Moral Philosophy Samuel Henley.

Dunmore left behind a letter to the Speaker in which he claimed to be the victim of a "blind and immeasurable fury [that had] unaccountably seized upon the minds and understanding of great numbers of the people."[115] Yet almost to a person, Virginians were shocked by his departure. Some even claimed to be hurt by it. Others recalled their surprise at seeing the Governor and his entire family sitting in the east gallery of Bruton Parish Church the evening before his flight. Like his predecessors, Dunmore had always used the governor's pew in the church's north aisle. The east gallery, which had its own covered stair to the outside, was normally used by students and slaves. It was now clear to everyone that the reason he had not used his pew that night was because he was afraid of being stopped.

For those who never wished him harm (still the majority of Virginians, including the many who felt sorry for his beautiful and dignified Lady for having to endure his many adulteries), his note to the Speaker citing "menaces and threats" by persons unnamed raised many questions. What threats? What else, besides rigging spring guns and planning his escape, had he been up to? Did his departure nullify Lord North's Olive Branch? Had Virginia, like it or not, been placed in a state of rebellion?[116]

These were not loose ends or idle questions. They implicated grave constitutional issues going to the power of a sitting governor to determine the terms and conditions of his office for himself. At the same time, he had left behind a badly-muddled

Bruton Parish Church as it looked in 1832
(the covered stairway to the outside can be seen in the right center of the picture).
"He was afraid of being stopped"

record on who was to blame for his ouster. There was a danger that his claim of being menaced would be accepted by what Jefferson called "a candid world" and a colony that had driven away its governor might find itself without good cause to revolt. There was something else: Virginians of all political persuasions liked to pride themselves on their loyalty, integrity and good sense. His Lordship's letter suggested that they had taken leave of all three.

For all these reasons, and in pursuit of the higher objective of unanimity, the House of Burgesses quickly concluded that matters could not be left to stand as they were. At the very least, they needed to investigate his Lordship's claim that he had been driven from office. To that end, an address was drawn up by a Committee of the Whole requesting that Dunmore reconsider his recent actions and offering measures "proper to the security of [him]self and family."[117] A delegation of six, including Dunmore's friend John Randolph and two Councilors (most likely Robert Carter III and Richard Corbin, who had tried to negotiate an end to the controversy earlier) waited on the Governor with a copy of the address. Two days later, on June 10, the House had his response: he refused "out of tenderness" to specify their menaces and threats and demanded that he be reinstated with full powers – a demand that might be taken to imply that he had been usurped.[118] "It is with real concern [Dunmore concluded] that I can discover nothing in your address that I think manifests the smallest inclination to, or will be productive of, a reconciliation with the mother country."[119]

Meanwhile, another House committee had issued a reply to Lord North's Olive Branch. Written by Thomas Jefferson (with no little interference from James Mercer and the Treasurer), it reflected, according to Jefferson, a minute study of North's proposal "in every point of light."[120] Because the Olive Branch only "change[d] the form of oppression without lightening its burthen," Jefferson concluded that neither he nor the House could "close with the terms." Unfortunately, a compromise that the House really liked, offered by William Pitt, had failed in Parliament. But even that was only a "basis for negotiation." It still had to be reconciled with the resolutions of the 1774 Congress. Somewhat disingenuously, Jefferson offered to lay North's offer before Congress, though, as he knew, the idea of treating with Congress was anathema to the Ministry. Like Dunmore's June 10 letter, Jefferson's reply to North's offer merely interposed new demands. In saying that Parliament had no right to meddle in Virginia's government, Jefferson was taking the old argument about lack of representation far beyond its former limits; in fact, he meant to avoid further negotiations. His discussion of "unjust taxation" is an example of this: "we alone [he said] are judges of [our] condition." What Jefferson wanted – though perhaps not a majority of the burgesses – was "a free station within the general system of the [British] Empire," not only for Virginia but for America. "What then remains to be done?" he asked rhetorically. The House had "exhausted itself" in efforts at compromise.

One thing that remained to be done was to reply to the Governor's June 10 letter. Stating definitively that it left no basis for further negotiations was one objective of this reply. Another – surely the more important one – was to place Dunmore's misdeeds and malfeasances on the historical record, thereby positioning him as the cause and instrument of his own ouster. Tasked with drafting this document, Robert Carter Nicholas began, predictably enough, with a hymn to Lord Botetourt of fond memory, who had given Virginia "Tranquility, and Happiness" even as he was striving to give the Ministry a "faithful Representation of Things, as he found them."[121] Having thus implied by comparison that Lord

Dunmore was a liar, Nicholas got down to cases. First came his point-by-point rebuttal of the recently-published "authentick Copy of Extracts of [his] Lordship's Letters to the same noble Earl [of Dartmouth], dated the 24th of December 1774." This was followed by an enumeration of the Governor's crimes (including his spring guns), then a recital (and rejection) of his Lordships' threats, including his "diabolical" threat to arm the slaves. It remained only to expose his lies, particularly the lie that he had been driven from office. Ironically, the best evidence to refute what Nicholas called Dunmore's "Fear of personal Danger" came from John Randolph, who recalled an "unmolested" Dunmore coming alone to his house the evening before his elopement. Nicholas concluded with an analysis of his Lordship's character and its effect on "a free People." Dunmore could never command respect. "[I]t must be a perfect Volunteer; and nothing is so likely to ensure it, to one in your Station, as Dignity of Character, and a candid and exemplary conduct." Having found Dunmore lacking in dignity, Nicholas called the question: "[I]f, after all, your Lordship is determined to persist in your Resolution of Absence we must endeavour to rest satisfied."

When the House of Burgesses recessed on June 24, it was with the prospect of war with Great Britain squarely in view. Even Richard Henry Lee was feeling a bit daunted. He walked out onto the porch of the Capitol building, and taking a pencil from his pocket, wrote the famous lines from the three witches in Shakespeare's *Macbeth* on one of the pillars:

> When shall we meet again?
> In thunder, lightning, and in rain;
> When the hurly-burly's done,
> When the battle's lost and won.[122]

The same day, a party of twenty-four gentlemen of the town broke into the Palace in broad daylight, took down the elaborate displays of muskets and swords in the hallway, counted them (there were actually 230 guns and 292 swords), and then carted them off to the Magazine. When the House met again on October 12, only 37 members showed up.[123] On March 7 of the following year, there were only 32.[124] On May 6, "Several members met, but did neither proceed to business nor adjourn as a House of Business."[125] Beneath this entry, in the precise hand that has endeared to him to generations of Williamsburg scholars, George Wythe wrote the word *"Finis."*[126] A flourish trailed off dreamily toward the margin, signifying a lingering doubt – or (perhaps) the unknown that lay ahead?[127]

Richard Henry Lee
"Even Richard Henry Lee was feeling a bit daunted"

The Revolution was on, and though it would be ascribed by historians to a principled dispute between enthusiasts for the British imperium on the one hand and lovers of liberty on the other, the very human impulses behind the idealogies and high-sounding phrases would get little airing. Nor would there be room for the view that Virginia's rebellion was largely the work of two men, each acting upon a belief in the inevitability of war, each determined to bring one on as soon as possible. For Dunmore, it would be about payback for ingratitude and a long list of personal rebuffs and humiliations beginning from the day he took office. For Patrick Henry, it would be about exploiting a tetchy, insecure governor's fears while making his face the face of British tyranny.

As to that, George Washington had a few thoughts which he wished to share with his friends. They should be required reading for anyone who thinks of Dunmore as a "joke" or who believes that Washington played no part in transforming Virginia's easy-going governor into a ferocious avenger of wrongs, both personal and public. "I do not mean to dictate," Washington told Congress, "I am sure [you] will pardon me for freely giving [you] my opinion, which is, that the fate of America a good deal depends on [Dunmore's] being obliged to evacuate Norfolk this winter."[128] To Joseph Reed he wrote, "If the Virginians are wise, that arch-traitor to the rights of humanity, Lord Dunmore, should be instantly crushed, if it takes the whole force of the colony to do it . . . But that which renders the measure indispensably necessary is the

One of Lord Dunmore's chairs, perhaps once occupied by George Washington

Negroes. For if he gets formidable, numbers will be tempted to join, who will be afraid to do it without."[129] A week later, in a letter to his old friend Richard Henry Lee, he advanced his demand for Dunmore's crushing to spring: "If my Dear Sir that Man [referring to Dunmore] is not crushed before Spring, he will become the most formidable Enemy America has – his strength will Increase as a Snow ball by Rolling . . . You will see by his Letters what pains he is taking to . . . translate the War to the Southern Colonies . . . nothing less than depriving him of life or liberty will secure peace to Virginia; as motives of Resentment actuate his conduct to a degree equal to the total destruction of the Colony."[130] Washington's last word on his one-time friend and would-be partner in land speculation was uttered in a note to his cousin Lund Washington: "[Should] one of our Bullets [be] A[i]med for . . . [Dunmore] the World would be happily rid of a Monster without any person sustaining a loss."[131]

That he placed first on Lord Dunmore's list of enemies Washington had little doubt. His August 20, 1775 letter to Lund Washington indicting Dunmore for seeking "revenge upon me [by] seiz[ing] Mrs Washington" is notable in many ways, and not least for his admission that Dunmore might have reason to be angry with him.[132] Still, why Dunmore should hate Washington enough to want to kidnap his wife is not easily explained. Washington's letters to Dunmore had always been respectful, while Dunmore's were warm and friendly, with one, on the death of Patcy Custis, evincing real pity for the same woman he now supposedly wanted to kidnap:[133]

WMBURG July 3d. 1773

Dear Sir

I received the favor of yours of the 20th of last Month on saturday last, as I did your former in April, & most certainly should have answered it then if I had not expected to be in your Neighborhood before your return from the North, & I then proposed to have waited upon you at Mount Vernon, where I was in hopes that we should have settled everything for our journey [to scout out land on the Ohio River]; but I am now most exceedingly sorry to learn by your last that you have so good a reason for changing your resolution, & I do sincerely condole with you, & poor Mrs. Washington for your loss [of Patcy], tho as the poor young Lady was so often afflicted with these fitts [of epilepsy], I dare say she thinks it a happy exchange [i.e., for heaven]. I propose to leave this [city] in a day or two in my way to Mr. Wormly's, to take up the Old Gentleman, who has promised to accompany me up to your part of the world, & if I thought it would not be disagreeable to Mrs. Washington I certainly would do myself the Honor of calling upon you, but if it should not be agreeable to Mrs. Washington to see company I hope I shall have the pleasure of meeting you at some of your Neighbor's which will oblige

> – your most Obt.
> – & very Hble. Sert.
> – DUNMORE

Augustine Prevost once described Dunmore as "unfit" but "by no means bad." For Dunmore, the badness of any action was always to be determined by its effect on himself. This is not to say that he was immoral or even amoral, only that he was self-centered and oddly fragile. At the top of his list of sins, implicating his own virtues and as well as his vices, was ingratitude. And this was Washington's offense in a nutshell. We will never know for sure what Dunmore and he talked about at his Lordship's hunting lodge on the York or on their boys' night out at the theater, but if the subject was land, how to find it and get it, the *quid pro quo* for Dunmore was loyalty. He was a tireless friend, albeit one that expected a return in affection, if not in profit. For Washington, it was simply about getting on Lord Dunmore's good side, and if he had to feign an interest in the Governor and his theories about how to fight the Indians, or join in the odd obscene toast (Dunmore was said to be fond of proposing toasts to female body parts), he was more than willing to do so.[134] In the process, he may have underestimated the effect of his friendship and imposing six-foot-three presence on a short, thin-skinned man with a deep need for acceptance and an even deeper need for friendship.

We might look for an answer in Washington's letters, except that he never wrote without an eye on history and was stopped from continuing to revise his diary only by death itself. Lord Dunmore's personal papers, those that survive, have yet to make it into the public domain. We are thus left with his official letters, specifically his December 24, 1774 letter to Dartmouth in which he recommended inflicting "distress and misery on these undutiful [Virginians]." But nameless offenses by undutiful Virginians hardly justified kidnapping Martha Washington. Apparently, Washington and Dunmore exchanged no letters during the year 1774. The only letter written by Washington to Dunmore during the following year, on April 3, 1775, concerns a rumor that Washington had heard to the effect that Dunmore's land grants to veterans of the French and Indian War, including himself, were now "null and void."[135] These were the same grants, issued over Dunmore's signature, that had nearly gotten the Governor fired. If Washington's letter sounded unusually querulous, if he placed too much emphasis on the "peculiar hardship" to himself, it might be because his strategy of secretly buying up the claims of other veterans was about to end in disaster. Dunmore's reply of April 18, 1775, just three days after his seizure of the gunpowder, is a model of cold, curt brevity. Unlike his July 3, 1773 letter it was addressed simply to

> Sir:
> I have received your letter dated the 3d. Instant. The information you have received that the Patents granted for the Lands under the Proclamation of 1754 would be declared Null and Void, is founded on a report that the Surveyor who Surveyed those Lands did not qualify agreeable to the Act of Assembly directing the duty and qualifications of Surveyors, if this is the Case the Patents will of Consequence be declared Null and Void.
> > I am Sir
> > –Your most Obedient
> > –humble Servant
> > –DUNMORE[136]

We may assume that the idea of disqualifying the surveyor

came from Dunmore (or Capt. Foy) ; that its aim was to undo his grants without raising doubts as to his power to make them in the first place; and that this note was meant to affirm the Governor, while putting the supplicant firmly in his place. As to that, we might paraphrase Robert Carter Nicholas (speaking of John Randolph) and say that though Washington had a "stock of virtues" he had allowed himself in this case to be "governed by interest"; and that when the rider from Fredericksburg called on him on April 26 to lead the militia in a march against the Palace, his interest had not shifted so far as to "draw [him] in a different Direction."* If that seems unfair, we need to remember that the standard Washington set for himself was high; that his four-year effort to make a friend of Dunmore made a mockery of his June 1768 declaration to Arthur Lee that he was ready to shoulder his musket against the British whenever his country called. It was Dunmore, not Washington, who was truest to himself in the last months before war broke out; Dunmore, not Washington, who was most loyal to his principles: "I do not perceive the misconduct which has made your lordship think . . . a caution necessary," [Dunmore had told Dartmouth], neither do I discover the justice of the heavy rebuke which your lordship communicates to me; and that I cannot avail myself of the plea of inadvertency which your lordship has put in my way, but that I think I must depend upon the integrity of my actions and the uprightness of my intentions for my justification."[137]

Had Virginians really no idea what made an enemy of their easy-going governor? Had they no regrets about their treatment of a man Virginius said was not "designed to shine in the

---

* See George T. Morrow, II, *Of Heretics, Traitors and True Believers* (Williamsburg, VA, 2011), p.52.

superior spheres of life, but [who] . . . if properly managed, might [be] exempt . . . from censure"? Hyper-sensitive as always to criticism, Dunmore must have seethed when he read Virginius' letter. Charges of "base corruption" and "murderer" were perhaps too grotesque to be believed in London. But the nasty condescension of "if properly managed" would be hard to bear for anyone, let alone an Earl (albeit a Scottish one) born to wealth and privilege and thus, literally entitled to deference. Dunmore's anger against the Virginians derived less from their portrayal of him as a roué or a tyrant than from the sense that he was the victim of outrageous condescension and monumental ingratitude. Whatever Virginius might say – truthfully – about his "low, unmanly, base evasions," "diabolical projects" and "corrupt heart," his Lordship had been more of an advocate for Virginia in its long territorial dispute with the colony of Pennsylvania than either Francis Fauquier or Lord Botetourt. Nor had any previous Governor been so bold (or so foolish) as to advocate an end to the slave trade. No one, certainly no governor of Virginia, had done more to assist Virginians in the pursuit of *their* self-interest.

The vengeance Dunmore chose, arming Virginians' own slaves, was no accident. He had told Hillsborough that the Spanish could easily take Virginia by freeing the slaves. And was not slavery the Virginians' greatest vunerability, in point of fact as well as in rhetoric? Notable in Dunmore's progress through the mazes of iniquity, from an easy, good-natured man to an Ethiop, was how that progress got registered in Virginians' minds. By 1775, his Lordship had reached the same metaphorical destination in thinking about Virginia as Virginius had reached in his indictment of Dunmore; the only difference was in their allegiances. Dunmore could think of nothing worse to *do* to Virginians than to unleash their slaves upon them. (As always, any real freedom enjoyed by Virginia's slaves would be in the fields of hyperbole.) But the paradoxes of slavery, in the fields and in metaphor, never really signified with Virginians. For them, the concept of moral legitimacy always took a backseat to the issue of moral authority. How could a corrupt tyrant who threatened them with a bloody race war be in the right – to which Dunmore might have replied (if he had had the chance) what better punishment for the drivers of slaves! Had he been able to fully carry through on his threat, Dunmore's payback for Virginia ingratitude might have given his royal masters the best argument – and army – they ever had against America's Revolution.

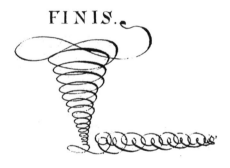

FINIS.

"Trailing dreamily off toward the margin"

Notes

1   Quoted in David Hackett Fischer, *Paul Revere's Ride* (Oxford, 1995), p.76.

2   Quoted in John E. Selby, *Dunmore*, (Williamsburg, VA, 1977), p.21.

3   *Revolutionary Virginia, The Road to Independence, A Documentary Record*, Robert L. Scribner, ed., (8 vols.; Charlottesville, VA, 1973), 3:100–101.

4   *Ibid.*, p.111.

5   Quoted in George Morgan, *The True Patrick Henry* (1905; reprint, Bridgewater, VA, 2000), pp.178–179, 179.

6   Earl of Dunmore to Earl of Dartmouth, 24 Dec. 1774, *Documents of the American Revolution, 1770–1783*, K.G. Davies, ed., (21 vols., Irish University Press, Shannon, 1972–81), 8: 267.

7   Andrew Burnaby, *Travels Through the Middle Settlements of North America in the Years 1759 and 1760*, (1798; reprint, Applewood Books, Carlisle, Mass.), pp.55–56.

8   *Virginia Gazette* (Pinckney), 29 Jun. 1775.

9   Quoted in Gordon S. Wood, *The Creation of the American Republic, 1776–1787* (Chapel Hill, NC, 1969, 1989), p.4. See also Edmund Randolph, History of Virginia (Charlottesville, VA, 1970), *passim.*

10   Percy B. Caley, "Dunmore: Colonial Governor of New York and Virginia," (Ph.D. Diss., Univ. of Pittsburgh, 1939), p.921.

11   Richard Henry Lee to Mrs. [Catherine] Macaulay, 29 Nov. 1775. "If Administration had searched thro' the world for a person best fitted to ruin their cause, they could not have found a more complete Agent than Lord Dunmore." *Letters of Richard Henry Lee*, James Curtis Ballagh, ed., (2 vols.; Charlottesville, VA, 1911–14), 1:162.

12   Selby, *Dunmore*, p.15. (Italics supplied.)

13   Quoted in Jane Carson, *James Innes and His Brothers of the F.H.C.* (Williamsburg, 1965), p.81.

14 Caley, *Dunmore: Colonial Governor of New York and Virginia*, p.321.

15 *Virginia Gazette* (Purdie and Dixon), 8 Dec. 1774, supp.

16 *Ibid.*

17 Quoted in Selby, *Dunmore*, p.19. See also, *Virginia Gazette* (Dixon and Hunter), 21 Jan. 1775.

18 Earl of Dunmore to Earl of Dartmouth, 24 Dec. 1774, *Documents of the American Revolution*, Davies, ed., 8: 267.

19 *Ibid.*

20 "Free THOUGHTS on the present TIMES and MEASURES, LETTER IV, To the PEOPLE of VIRGINIA," by Virginius, *Virginia Gazette* (Pinckney), 29 Jun. 1775.

21 Randolph, *History of Virginia*, p.197.

22 George Washington to Richard Henry Lee, 27 Nov. 1775, *The Papers of George Washington: Revolutionary War Series*, W.W. Abbott, Dorothy Twohig, Philander D. Chase, Edward G. Lengel and David R. Hoth, eds., (18 vols., Charlottesville, VA 1985–), 2:436; George Washington to Richard Henry Lee, 26 Dec. 1775, *The Writings of George Washington From The Original Sources: Volume 4*, Electronic Text Center, Univ. of Virginia Library, http://etext.virginia.edu/etcbin/toccer-new2?id=Was Fi04.xml&images=images/modeng&data=/texts/english/modeng/par sed&tag=public&part=169&division =div1 (accessed 12/15/2011).

23 Nicholas B. Wainwright, ed., "Turmoil at Pittsburgh, Diary of Augustine Prevost, 1774," *The Pennsylvania Magazine of History and Biography*, (April, 1961), 85: 111–161, 143.

24 John Connolly to George Washington, 29 Aug. 1773, *George Washington's Papers at the Library of Congress*, http://memory.loc.gov/cgi-bin/query/r?ammem/mgw:@field(DOCID+@lit(lw040146)) (accessed 12 Dec. 2011). See also, John Connolly to George Washington, 1 Feb. 1774, *ibid.*, http://memory.loc.gov/cgi-bin/query/r? ammem/mgw:@field(DOCID+@lit(lw040180)) (accessed 12 Dec. 2011) and John Connolly to George Washington, 19 Jun. 1773, ibid., http://memory.loc.gov/cgi-bin/query/r?ammem/mgw:@field (DOCID +@lit(lw040126)) (accessed 12 Dec. 2011).

25 Earl of Dunmore to George Washington, 3 Jul.1773, *The George Washington Papers at the Library of Congress*, http://memory.loc.gov/cgi-bin/query/r?ammem/mgw:@field (DOCID+@lit(lw040132)) (accessed

12/15/2011).

26 The long, complicated story of Dunmore's efforts to enrich himself and his friend, George Washington, with grants of Virginia land is discussed in detail in Caley, *Dunmore: Colonial Governor of New York and Virginia*, pp 145–210 See also, Selby, *Dunmore*, p.14, in which Selby notes that Dunmore "put in a claim for 20,000 acres for each of his five sons, plus 10,000 for his aide, Capt. Foy."

27 Quoted in Caley, *Dunmore, Colonial Governor of New York and Virginia*, p.185. In this connection, see also Washington's November 2, 1773 letter to Dunmore seeking to persuade him to set aside both his instructions (and his own reservations) and make new grants of land in the west. George Washington to Lord Dunmore, 2 Nov. 1773, Account Book, *The George Washington Papers at the Library of Congress, 1741–1799.* http://memory.loc.gov/cgi-bin/query/r?ammem/mgw:@ field(DOCID+@lit(gwo30128)) (accessed 12/16/2011).

28 Wainwright, ed., "Turmoil at Pittsburgh," 85:138,141. The charge that Dunmore was a habitual drunkard seems to rest primarily on the large quantity of wine and spirits found in the Palace after his departure. But if this anecdote is any indication, Dunmore held his liquor better than his drinking companions.

29 *Ibid.*, 85:140, 141 fn., 91,136,137,142,143. On Dunmore preying on the weaknesses of other men, see Randolph, *History of Virginia*, p.196.

30 Selby, *Dunmore*, p.2.

31 Earl of Dartmouth to the Earl of Dunmore, 8 Sept. 1774, *Documents*, 8: 194. Before sending off the reprimand, Dartmouth sent a copy of it to Dunmore's patron and brother-in-law, Earl Gower, and asked his opinion. In a letter dated 4 Sept. 1774, Gower told Dartmouth that he thought the "enclos'd draft . . . both proper and necessary." He declined to take upon himself the task of writing "purposely upon the subject to [Dunmore]," though he did promise to "throw in a hint to him upon the matter" when an opportunity offered. Earl Gower to Lord Dartmouth, 4 Sep. 1774, Document (w) 1778/11/957, Staffordshire Record Office, Stafford.

32 Earl of Dunmore to Earl of Dartmouth, 16 May 1774, *Documents*, 8:113–115.

33 Earl of Dartmouth to Earl of Dunmore, 8 Sept. 1774, *Documents*,

8:195.

34 *Ibid.* It would take a book to detail all of the manoeuverings of these two companies. Suffice it to say that the members of the Walpole Company (which included Benjamin Franklin) had offered the members of the Ohio Company two shares in the Walpole Company in return for abandoning their application. George Mercer, the Ohio Company's London lobbyist, was offered the job of President of the Walpole Company.

35 *Ibid.*, 8:195–196.

36 Earl of Dunmore to Earl of Dartmouth, 24 Dec. 1774, *Documents*, 8:252.

37 *Ibid.*, p.255.

38 *Ibid.*, pp.252, 257. Standing on the uprightness of his intentions was perhaps going a bit far. But it was characteristic of Dunmore that whenever he was discovered in a lie or found to have acted improperly, he tended to fall back on his good intentions, not the intentions he actually had (which *were* bad), but the intentions he *should have had*. Were he to be challenged he could say – truthfully – that he *aspired* to do the right thing. The problem was that he aspired from a lot further back than most people, and seldom *did* the right thing, unless it was to suit himself.

39 Earl of Dunmore to Earl of Dartmouth, 24 Dec. 1774, *Documents*, 8:266–267.

40 Earl of Dunmore to Earl of Hillsborough, 2 May 1772, *Documents*, 5:96; Earl of Dunmore to Earl of Dartmouth, 16 Nov. 1772; *Documents*, 5:220–223 .

41 *Journal of House of Burgesses 1770–1772*, John Pendleton Kennedy, ed. (1906; reprint, Heritage Books, 1996), Tuesday the 18th of February, 1772, pp.171–173, 173 and Monday, the 24th of February, 1772, pp.185–187, 185.

42 The affair of the kidnapped forgers is discussed at length in Caley, *Dunmore: Colonial Governor of New York and Virginia*, pp.132–138. Dunmore's reply to the House's rebuke can be found on p 137. The sarcasm about "the most timid" was directed at Patrick Henry.

43 Earl of Dunmore to Earl of Hillsborough, 1 May 1772, *Documents*, 5:94. In their haste to condemn Dunmore the barbarian, Virginians were

quick to forget the friend who had taken their side in an argument that the was sure to lose. That Dunmore's observation was the father of the idea of using slaves as an army of retribution is an interesting, if unprovable, proposition.

44   Earl of Dunmore to Earl of Dartmouth, 20 Mar. 1774, *Documents* 8: 69. See also, Earl of Dunmore to Earl of Dartmouth, 9 Jul. 1773, *Documents*, 5:182.

45   Earl of Dunmore to Earl of Dartmouth, 24 Dec. 1774, *Documents*, 8:267.

46   *Boswell's Life of Johnson*, George Birkbeck Hill, ed. (6 vols.; Oxford, 1950), 1:408.

47   *Ibid.*, 2: 219.

48   *Journal of the House of Burgesses*, 1770–1772, pp.154–155, 154.

49   Earl of Dunmore to Earl of Dartmouth, 24 Dec. 1774, *Documents*, 8: 269.

50   *Ibid.*, 8: 267.

51   Wirt, *Sketches of The Life and Character of Patrick Henry*, (Richmond, Va. 1817; Reprint, Messenger Pub. Co) p.105.

52   *Ibid.*, p.104, said to be on the "the authority" of Col. Richard Morris and Capt. George Dabney.

53   *Ibid.*, p.73, quoting from a letter to Wirt from John Pope. See also, William Wirt Henry, *Patrick Henry, Life, Correspondence and Speeches*, (3 vols.; New York, 1891), 1: 207–208.

54   Chiswell's body was brought to Scotchtown for burial. Unconvinced that he was dead, Routledge's friends insisted that his coffin be opened so they could see for themselves. This was done, Chiswell was found to be as dead as dead can be and the funeral went forward.

55   Quoted in Robert Douthat Meade, *Patrick Henry: Patriot in the Making* (Philadelphia, 1957), p.281.

56   Afficionados of Charlotte Brontë's *Jane Eyre* (1847) may notice resemblances between Sallie Henry's keeper and the the clearly overwrought jailer of Bertha Rochester. Coincidental though these similarities may be, they are highly suggestive of Henry's state of mind and so worth quoting: "'One night I had been awakened by her yells – (since the medical men had pronounced her mad, she had of course been shut up) – it was a fiery West Indian night; one of the

description that precedes the hurricanes of those climates; being unable to sleep in bed, I got up and opened the window. The air was like sulphur-streams – I could find no refreshment anywhere. Mosquitoes came buzzing in and hummed sullenly round the room, the sea, which I could hear from thence, rumbled dull like an earthquake – black clouds were casting up over it; the moon was setting in the waves, broad and red, like a cannon-ball – she threw her last bloody glance over a world quivering with the ferment of tempest. I was physically influenced by the atmosphere and scene, and my ears were filled with the curses the maniac still shrieked out; wherein she momentarily mingled my name with such a tone of demon-hate, with such language! – no professed harlot ever had a fouler vocabulary than she; though two rooms off, I heard every word – the thin partitions of the West India house opposing but slight obstruction to her wolfish cries.'" Charlotte Brontë, *Jane Eyre* (New York, 1864), p.326.

57 Freely translated from the Latin motto above the front entrance to "Auchinleck," the 18th Century country house built by James Boswell's father in Ayrshire, Scotland: "*Quod petis hic est, Est Ulubris, animus sit e non deficit aequus.*"

58 Henry's speech was given in support of some amendments he proposed to add to a resolution destined for the General Assembly of Jamaica, thanking it for its help. Needless to say, the still-loyal Jamaicans were unlikely to take much joy in the news that Virginia was being "put into a posture of defence; and that . . . a committee [was being appointed] to prepare a plan for embodying, arming and disciplining . . . a number of men as may be sufficient for that purpose." Morgan, *The True Patrick Henry*, p.183.

59 Wirt, *Sketches*, pp.93–95.

60 Quoted in William Wirt Henry, *Patrick Henry*, 1: 265.

61 Quoted in Morgan, *The True Patrick Henry*, pp.194–195.

62 *Ibid.*, p.184.

63 The reactions of Nicholas, Carrington, the elderly Baptist minister and Nelson can all be found in *Revolutionary Virginia*, 2: 369, fn. 8.

64 There is some dispute about this, as only 118 members were present and entitled to vote. See *Revolutionary Virginia*, 2: 369, fn. 8.

65 Patrick Henry found Pendleton too aristocratic. Other, perhaps less

prejudiced observers, described the blue-eyed, white-maned lawyer as the most elegant orator in Virginia. He certainly had married well. As the son-in-law of Speaker John Robinson, Pendleton's rise in the House of Burgesses seemed inevitable, until Robinson died and it was discovered that he had bankrupted the colony by making loans from the colony's retired currency to improvident planters. After that, Pendleton had to make his own way, which he did very well, becoming an expert in the use of process to kill legislation he opposed. It would be easy – but wrong – to view him as Henry's foil in law, politics and society. In fact, both men were highly successful, largely self-taught lawyers. But while Henry seemed to enjoy the life of a country squire at Scotchtown, Pendleton defied expectation by living rather simply in a frame house ("Edmundsbury") in rural Caroline County. While Henry was famously careless of his dress, Pendleton was stylish in lawyer black; and while Henry was popular with the people, Pendleton was affable but remote. He also hated change. In the debate over Henry's amendment, Pendleton maintained that it would bring conflict on sooner – which of course was exactly what Henry wanted.

66 Morgan, *The True Patrick Henry*, p.193.
67 Much more could be said on this point: the link between "helplessness and agony"; the "distortion" of Henry's face by "agony and rage"; the "heartbroken, hopeless felon" who commits suicide (or is it murder?) – all suggest a deeply-conflicted man enacting his release from emotional captivity. It was still a speech about the need for an army and the inevitability of war. Yet, in the way of all good orators and actors, Henry was drawing on his own feelings to lend urgency to his portrayal of the condemned galley slave breaking his bonds.
68 Quoted in Ivor Noel Hume, *1775: Another Part Of The Field* (New York, 1966), p.119.
69 *Virginia Gazette* (Dixon and Hunter), 1 Apr. 1775.
70 Randolph, *History of Virginia*, p.214.
71 Lord Dunmore to the Earl of Dartmouth, 25 June. 1775, *Documents*, 9: 207–208.
72 Morgan, *The True Patrick Henry*, p.192. The commentator was Moses Coit Tyler (1835–1900), author of *Patrick Henry* (Cambridge, Mass.,

1887).

73 "Royal Chief Magistracy, Governor Dunmore to His Council, May 2, 1775," *Revolutionary Virginia*, 3:77. (In his April 29, 1775 *Gazette*, Alexander Purdie had declared "The *sword is now drawn*, and *God* knows when it will be sheathed.")

74 Though Dunmore had by now received Dartmouth's March 3 reply to his letter of December 24, 1774, assuring him that his explanation for making grants of land left "no room in the royal breast to doubt the uprightness of [his] intentions," he was never one to forget what he viewed as an unjust rebuke. If anything, as events would show, his resentment was likely to grow, giving way at last to furious over-reaction. See The Earl of Dartmouth to Lord Dunmore, 3 Mar. 1775, *Documents*, 9: 62.

75 Lord Dunmore to the Earl of Dartmouth,1 May 1775, *Documents*, 9: 108.

76 Lord Dunmore to the Earl of Dartmouth, 25 Jun.1775, *Documents*, 9: 201. James Parker was not impressed. "These Shirt men, or Virginia uniform, are dressed with an Oxnab[rig, i.e., linen] Shirt over their Cloaths, a belt round them with a Tommy hawk & Scalping Knife. They look like a band of Assassins & it is my opinion if they fight at all it will be that way. Another observer described the usually cheerful Clerk of the House of Burgesses as "grim-faced." Quoted in Hume, *1775*, p.179.

77 See "Introductory Note," *Revolutionary Virginia*, p.5.

78 See "The Capital, Municipal Common Hall to Govenor Dunmore, An Humble Address," *Revolutionary Virginia*, 3: 54. "Governor Dunmore to the Municipal Common Hall. An Oral Reply," *Ibid.*, p.55. For Dunmore's own account of Collins' raid and his explanation of his motives, see Lord Dunmore to the Earl of Dartmouth, 1 May 1775, *Documents*, 9: 108.

79 *Executive Journals of the Council of Colonial Virginia*, H. R. McIlwaine and Benjamin J. Hillman, eds., (6 vols.; Richmond Va, 1925–1966) 6: 580.

80 *Virginia Gazette* (Dixon and Hunter), 6 May 1775.

81 Lord Dunmore to the Earl of Dartmouth, 1 May 1775, *Documents*, 9: 108; John Page, "Autobiographical Reminiscences," quoted in

Carson, *James Innes and His Brothers of the F.H.C.*, p.81.

82 In his final "Report of the Committee on the Causes of the Late Disturbances and Commotions," (read to the House of Burgesses on the 19th of June, 1775), Committee Chairman Robert Carter Nicholas went to some lengths to distinguish the conduct of "the truly noble Lord Botetourt" from his successor. Chief among Botetourt's virtues was "his exemplary Conduct, in all respects." Chief among Dunmore's defects was his failure to remember that "Respect . . . is not to be obtained by Force, from a free People." In noting that respect "must be a perfect Volunteer; and nothing is so likely to ensure it, to one in your Station, as Dignity of Character, [and] . . . candid and exemplary Conduct," Nicholas put his finger on the problem, while distancing himself from Dunmore's Whig critics. Dunmore's problem was not simply that he had behaved tyranically; it was that he lacked dignity. *Journal of the House of Burgesses*, Monday, the 19th of June, p.254. (On Dunmore's womanizing, see George Morrow, *A Cock and Bull for Kitty* (Williamsburg, VA, 2011.))

83 "Draft Report of the Committee on the Causes of the Late Disturbances and Commotions," *Journal of the House of Burgesses in Virginia, 1773–1776*, 14th of June, 1775, pp.227–237, 231, 232–233.

84 Earl of Dunmore to Earl of Dartmouth, 1 May 1775, *Documents*, 9: 108.

85 "Draft Report of the Committee on the Causes of the Late Disturbances and Commontions," *Journal of the House of Burgesses in Virginia, 1773–1776*, 14th of June, p.231.

86 *Ibid.*

87 *Ibid.*, p.232.

88 *Ibid.*

89 See final "Report of the Committee on the Causes of the Late Disturbances and Commotions," *Journal of the House of Burgesses*, the 19th of June, p.258.

90 *The Papers of George Washington, Diaries*, Donald Jackson and Dorothy Twohig, eds. (6 vols.; Charlottesville, VA, 1978), 3: 320.

91 Peyton Randolph to Mann Page, Jr. et. al,, 27 Apr. 1775, *Revolutionary Virginia*, 3: 63–64; *Diaries*, 2: 193. "Spotsylvania Council, Pledge of Readiness at a Moment's Warning," *Revolutionary Virginia*, 3:70–71.

92 Final "Report of the Committee on the Causes of the Late Distur-

bances and Commotions," *Journal of the House of Burgesses*, Monday, the 19th of June, p.258

93   Wirt, *Sketches*, p.105.

94   *Ibid.*, pp.105–106.

95   Estimates of the number of men said to have joined Henry on his march to Williamsburg vary from 150 to 5,000, the latter number being supplied by Wirt, who thought it low at that, perhaps because he included those who were still "crossing the country to crowd around" Henry's standard. See *Revolutionary Virginia*, 3: 8.

96   Late on the night of May 3 – about the time Henry was receiving his check – Dunmore sent a note to Capt. Montagu of the H.M.S. *Fowey* at Yorktown, saying that he was "threatened with attack at daybreak," and asking Montague to send him a detachment of British marines. As it was 13 miles to Williamsburg and as his Lordship's message did not arrive until very late, Montagu decided to see what he could accomplish with a salvo of *verbal* bombast, an idea perhaps suggested to him by his fine view of the city's skyline from the river. There, within easy range of the *Fowey's* guns, stood the elegant brick house of Thomas Nelson Jr., a firm Whig, and what is more, a man of great influence among the Virginians. The logic was worthy of a Dunmore: Montagu would repel Patrick Henry at Williamsburg by bombarding the city of Yorktown.

> Sir [Montagu wrote Nelson], – I have this morning received certain information that his excellency Lord Dunmore, governor of Virginia, is threatened with an attack at daybreak, this morning, at his palace in Williamsburg, and have thought proper to send a detachment from his majesty's ship under my command, to support his excellency; therefore strongly pray you to make use of every endeavor to prevent the party from being molested and attacked, as in that case I must be under a necessity to fire upon this town. *Revolutionary Virginia*, 3:91.

For "threatening to bombard the defenseless town of Yorktown," the Yorktown Council honored Montagu as man of "unprecedented [cruelty] in the annals of civilized times" Wirt, *Sketches*, p.110. A different honor was reserved for his marines, who did manage to reach

Williamsburg by marching all night, only to then tumble "into a ditch" behind the Palace. The farcical result was not all their fault. His Lordship had insisted that they douse their lanterns before entering the Palace grounds so as not to be observed.

97   Wirt, *Sketches*, p.108. The full text of the note is as follows, "Received from the Honorable Richard Corbin, Esq., his majesty's receiver-general, three hundred and thirty pounds, as a compensation for the gunpowder lately taken out of the public magazine by the governor's order; which money I promise to convey to the Virginia delegates at the general congress, to be, under their direction, laid out in gunpowder for the colony's use, and to be stored as they shall direct, until the next colony convention, or general assembly; unless it shall be necessary, in the meantime, to use the same in the defense of this colony. It is agreed, that in case the next convention shall determine that any part of the said money ought to be returned to the majesty's said receiver-general, that the same shall be done accordingly."

98   *Ibid.*, 110–111.

99   *Virginia Gazette* (Dixon and Hunter), 13 May 1775. (Italics in the original.)

100   "Draft Report of the Committee on the Causes of the Late Disturbances and Commotions," *Journal of the House of Burgesses*, Wednesday, the 14th of June, pp.231–237, 232.

101   Wirt, *Sketches*, p.112.

102   *Ibid.*, p.109.

103   *Virginia Gazette* (Dixon and Hunter), 29 Apr. 1775, (Supp.),

104   Earl of Dunmore to Earl of Dartmouth, 1 May 1775, *Documents*, 9: 109.

105   *Virginia Gazette* (Dixon and Hunter), 20 May 1775.

106   William Shakespeare, *Anthony and Cleopatra*, Act I, Scene 5.

107   *Journal of the House of Burgesses*, Tuesday, the 13th of June, p.223.

108   *Virginia Gazette* (Purdie), 9 Jun. 1775.

109   As Virginus put it, "Can any confidence be reposed in a murderer? I know not how your lordship could reconcile to your feelings the idea of the *secret assassin*, the *dark murderer*. But I believe there are very few who do not rank you in that class. I care not whether the incautious, but brave young fellows, who have fallen victim to your dark plans, have expired of their wounds or not; it is the intention of the agent

that should regulate our judgment of any actions; and here you stand self-convicted. Will you then confess that evil counselors, and pernicious advisers, betrayed you into that diabolical project? Or that it was the machination of your own corrupt heart? Deviate, I conjure you, for once, into *candour*." "Free THOUGHTS on the present TIMES and MEASURES, LETTER IV, To the PEOPLE of VIRGINIA," *Virginia Gazette* (Pinckney), 29 Jun. 1775,

110 *Virginia Gazette* (Dixon and Hunter) 3 Jun. 1775. In fact, they printed their report of the incident immediately following their report of the Governor's presentation of Lord North's olive branch – thereby raising a fair question as to whether an offer of compromise conveyed by a man who resorted to spring guns could be trusted.

111 Pitt, as quoted in William Wirt Henry, *Patrick Henry* p.273.

112 *Virginia Gazette* (Pinckney), 1 Jun. 1775.

113 *Virginia Gazette* (Dixon and Hunter), 3 Jun. 1775. Any sum (the term "tax" was used by way of contrast) "freely" offered by Virginia to offset public burdens along with "justice, equity and moderation" in their proposals, would be taken as a mark of "duty and attachment to their sovereign" and as "a testimony of reverence" to Parliament.

114 *Virginia Gazette* (Pinckney), 1 Jun. 1775; *Virginia Gazette*, (Dixon and Hunter) 3 Jun. 1775.

115 *Journal of the House of Burgesses*, Thursday, the 8th of June, p.206.

116 See *Virginia Gazette* (Pinckney), 15 Jun. 1775

117 *Journal of the House of Burgesses*, Thursday, the 8th of June, p.207.

118 *Journal of the House of Burgesses*, Saturday, the 10th of June, pp.214–215.

119 *Journal of the House of Burgesses in Virginia*, 1773–1776, Friday, the 16th of June, p.245.

120 *Journal of the House of Burgesses*, Friday, the 10th of June, pp.212–214 (Jefferson's draft) and 219–221 (the final version.)

121 Final "Report of the Committee on the Causes of the Late Disturbances and Commotions," *Journal of the House of Burgesses*, Monday, the 19th of June, pp.253–262, 258.

122 William Shakespeare, *Macbeth*, Act I, Scene 1.

123 *Journal of the House of Burgesses*, Thursday, the 12th of October, p.283.

124 *Ibid.*

125 *Ibid.*

126 *Ibid.*

127 *Ibid.*

128 George Washington to the President of Congress, 18 Dec. 1775, *The Writings of George Washington,* Worthington Chauncey Ford, ed., (New York, 1889), http://hdl.handle.net/2027/mdp.39015051654724?urlappend=%3Bseq=307 (accessed 1/31/2012).

129 George Washington to Joseph Reed, 15 Dec. 1775, *ibid.,* http://hdl.handle.net/2027/mdp.39015051654724?urlappend=%3Bseq=303 (accessed 1/31/2012).

130 George Washington to Richard Henry Lee, 26 Dec. 1775, *ibid.,* http://hdl.handle.net/2027/mdp.39015051654724?urlappend=%3Bseq=322 (accessed 1/31/2012).

131 George Washington to Lund Washington, 20 Aug. 1775, *Papers, Revolutionary War Series,* 1:335–36.

132 *Ibid.*

133 Lord Dunmore to George Washington, 3 Jul. 1773, *George Washington's Papers at the Library of Congress,* http://memory.loc.gov/cgi-bin/query/r?ammem/mgw:@field(DOCID+@lit (lw040132))3 (accessed 1/25/2012.)

134 James A. Hagemann, *Lord Dunmore, Last Royal Governor of Virginia, 1771–1776* (Hampton, VA, 1774), p. 2.

135 George Washington to Lord Dunmore, 3 Apr. 1775, *The Writings of George Washington from the Original Manuscript Sources,* http://memory.loc.gov/cgi-bin/query/r?ammem/mgw:@field(DOCID+@lit(gwo30201)) (accessed 1/31/2012.)

136 Lord Dunmore to George Washington, 18 Apr. 1775, *George Washington Papers at the Library of Congress,* http://memory. loc. gov/cgi-bin/query/r?ammem/mgw:@field(DOCID+@lit(lw050098)) (accessed 1/31/2012).

137 Lord Dunmore to Lord Dartmouth, 24 Dec. 1774, *Documents,* 8:252.

"War!"

The progress of a lie to a damn lie is – or ought to be – the stuff of history. This would seem especially true if the lie is part of the rationale for a nation's existence. When Samuel Adams learned that Lord Dunmore had Norfolk put to the torch, he wrote to his friend Joseph Warren, "This will prevail more than a long train of Reasoning to accomplish a Confederation, and other Matters which I know your heart as well as mine is much set upon." When Gen. Washington heard about it, he predicted that the action would become a "flaming argument . . . that will not leave numbers at a loss to decide upon . . . separation" from Britain. He was right. When the time came for Jefferson to make America's case to "a candid world," the razing of Norfolk was given a featured place in the recital of wrongs attributed to George III. It was a lie that was fated to send down very deep roots into the mythic landscape of this country – so deep, that despite having been officially certified as a lie in 1777 (though the truth would not be published to the world until 1835), historians of the Revolution in Virginia continue to charge Dunmore with having burned Norfolk, down to "every last house."

Meanwhile, a home grown plot against Patrick Henry has gone all but undetected. That one of the plotters was also the arsonist of Norfolk, Col. William Woodford, Jr., and that Woodford was in league with Henry's arch enemy, Edmund Pendleton, is more than an irony. It is proof, historically speaking, that Virginia's revolution was never in the hands of radicals. It was in the hands of the moderates and conservatives on Pendleton's Safety Committee or in the hands of Convention delegates, many of them burgesses from the old colonial Assembly. It was also in the hands of men who had served, like Woodford, in the French and Indian War. This state of affairs would change over the course of time as the old order in Virginia died off and less inhibited back country rebels emerged to take its place in the councils of power. But one effect of this situation was to make Virginia's revolution seem more like a work in progress; a revolution which, as George Mason said, kept undoing one day what it did the day before – a revolution which paradoxically viewed the most ardent rebel in America as a potential dictator.

It is safe to say that Henry would never have approved of the razing of Norfolk. While the record is silent as to what he said when he heard the truth about Norfolk, it speaks volumes as to Henry's basic decency and sense of honor. Woodford's own explanation for razing the city of Norfolk failed to meet the test of credulity, while his enmity toward the inhabitants, particularly the hated Scots merchants, of whom he and his co-commander, Col. William Howe, had "the worst opinion", is a matter of record. Here was the usual justice of the victor to the helpless rendered under the excuse of military necessity. Were it otherwise, it might have been disclosed to a candid world. But what would a candid world have said of a people who razed an entire city because it was inhabited by "suspicious *friends?*"

The plot against Patrick Henry was inspired by fear – fear that he would use his powerful oratory and influence within the army to make himself dictator of Virginia. Instead, he used its influence to put down an uprising of his army, incensed by Pendleton's humiliating treatment of their Commander in Chief. That Henry chose not to seize control of Virginia's wandering rebellion was typical of the man, not of the spell-binding orator, but of a man prepared to set aside pride and legitimate misgivings for the cause. Was he disabled by his sense of duty? Was he afflicted with doubts about his military ability? Was he thinking of running for Governor, a position which would not exist until May, 1776, but which he had every reason to believe might be his on the basis that the Convention "owed him one" for what he had had to endure as Virginia's Commander in Chief? Let us say that Henry, like Washington, had an instinct for greatness – and the grace to simply let it happen.

Perhaps the very opposite could be said for the villain in the piece, Lord Dunmore. Having seen off his lady and children and friend John Randolph over the course of the summer; having given his blessing to Capt. Foy's oft-expressed wish to "have done with Lord Dunmore;" and having sent off Kitty Eustace's brother John to General Howe in Boston with a glowing letter of recommendation, his Lordship was more alone and more at odds with himself than perhaps at any time in his life. He was not exaggerating when he told Dartmouth he did not have "a living soul to consult with." Nor did he have more "cheap courtesies," as Edmund Randolph called the benefits he was in the habit of conferring on his friends in return for personal favors. Having been "imprisoned" on a ship "between eight or nine months," he was ready for a change. His outrage on hearing that the British force of 1000 men and six ships which sailed into Hampton on February 18 was designated for the Carolinas rather than Virginia was enormous. We know that because he put it into a postscript to a letter to Dartmouth announcing the fleet's arrival:

This moment General Clinton is arrived, and to my inexpressible mortification [I] find that he is ordered by your lordship to North Carolina, a most insignificant province, when this, which is the first colony on the continent both for its riches and power, is [he had apparently forgotten what he said about Virginia in his letters to Lord Hillsborough in 1771] totally neglected. Had North Carolina been your object, policy in my poor opinion ought to have induced your lordship to have ordered your army to have rendezvoused here for many reasons, first because this is a safe harbour both for access and riding in, where pilots are to be got, the other very difficult of access even for vessels of small burthen and not a pilot to be had, and when in, a very unsafe roadstead. Besides this, any little knowledge I have of military operations has ever induced me to think it prudent to conceal as long as possible your real intentions from your enemy. Which cannot happen here because it is impossible to expect that force coming from so many different quarters can all arrive at the same time or even near it; therefore, the enemy will have time to collect and prepare themselves.

His admission of "little knowledge of military operations" represented a rare moment of candor. It was also true. "To see my government thus totally neglected [he told Dartmouth], . . . is a mortification I was not prepared to meet with after being imprisoned on board a ship between eight and nine months, and now left without a hope of relief either to myself or the many unhappy friends of government that are now afloat suffering with me, but I have done." The letter was signed "DUNMORE," the short form of his name and the capital letters meant to signify his outrage.

He was not done of course. Though he was now forced to throw "30 fine fellows [slaves]" overboard every night due to death from disease, he could not simply give up the fight. Not only his army of Ethiopians, but thousands of men, women and children, loyalists all depended on him. It was he who had eloped from his office; he who had threatened to reduce the city of Williamsburg to ashes, he who had formed an army, a large part of which were slaves, and placed Virginia in rebellion. He was looked upon as a savior, but a savior who had led his people to disaster. How could he not stand by them?

He was not a moral man. But he did have a strong sense of loyalty. Even those who despised him – people like Capt. Foy and John Skey Eustace – were prepared to concede that. He was not an honest man. But he was an affable, energetic and, within his limits, dutiful man. No one had asked him to stay in Virginia; if anything, Gen. Clinton's arrival was his clear signal to leave. But leaving would have meant abandoning all that had brought him to America in the first place, not only the emoluments, but all the hopes (and some of the fears) that went with serving his king. With a few more ships, a larger army and better luck, he might yet restore Virginia to the crown. But the fault (as Hamlet says) was not in his stars. It was in him. If he had known that he was about to face an even greater disaster at a place called Gwynn's Island, would he have then fled to New York? It seems unlikely. He was no coward, and he was determined to do his duty, determined to exert himself for friends like Capt. Foy and John Skey Eustace long after they had abandoned him. He never did have good judgment.

Acknowledgements

Dr. Samuel Johnson once said, "It is wonderful how a man will sometimes turn over half a library to make just one book." After ten years of nearly constant work on this series, I find that I have not only turned over half a library, but a good part of my life. New friends have become old ones. Some very good friends who read the essays in this series in their very earliest versions are now gone. Meanwhile, the library – I am speaking of the ever-expanding library of the internet – has only gotten larger.

It is impossible to name everyone who helped make this series, but some I must mention. There would be no series without the love, encouragement and help of my wife, Joan Morrow. But for the welcoming attitude, expert assistance and criticism of two truly fine historians of the period, Rhys Isaac and James Horn, I would still be trying to distinguish the forest from the trees. The encouragement I received from my two chief non professional readers, Joan and Terry Thomas, turned a mere collection of dates, people and events into a study of the character of Williamsburg. Other people who read one or more of the essays and made helpful comments include my 90-year-old aunt Rosemary Bauder, Paul and Joan Wernick, Richard Schumann, Bill Barker, Michael Fincham, Ken and Judith Simmons, Fred Fey, Cary Carson, Jon Kite, Al Louer, Bob Hill and Collen Isaac. I also wish in particular to thank Jon Kite for obtaining the French army dossier of John Skey Eustace and for translating one of Jack Eustace's overwrought pamphlets from the French. Richard Schumann, James Horn and Roger Hudson kindly consented to do prefaces for one of the booklets in this series. Al Louer and Paul Freiling of Colonial Williamsburg arranged for me to see Williamsburg from the roof of the Governor's Palace, a view that put time itself in perspective .

Those who are subscribers to the British quarterly, *Slightly Foxed*, described on its website as "The Real Reader's Quarterly," will recognize some similarities between the booklets in this series and that magazine. The resemblance is no accident. When I saw *Slightly Foxed* for the first time, I immediately realized that it was the perfect model, in size, material and design for what I was looking for. With that in mind, I contacted Andrew Evans at 875 Design, the English book design firm responsible for its appearance, and asked him if would be willing to take on this project. He said, "yes," and it was not long before he and I had assembled a team of people who not only seemed to know what I wanted but were able to give me something I never expected to find: new ideas on the subject matter. I especially want to thank Gail Pirkis, the publisher of *Slightly Foxed*, for recommending Roger Hudson as editor for this series. Roger is not only a highly accomplished writer in his own right, he is truly a writer's editor.

Sadly, the genial spirit who presided over the series, read and commented on virtually every booklet and guided me through its development, died while the series was still in production. I am speaking of Rhys Isaac, the Pulitzer Prize-winning author of what is still the best book ever written on late colonial Virginia, *The Transformation of Virginia*. Rhys' presence at our dinner table will be deeply missed. But he will also be missed from the profession of history, where his exuberant writing style and elegiac approach to the past daily gave the lie to the sour souls who think history is about settling scores.

As I began these Acknowledgments with a quotation from

Samuel Johnson I would like to end with one *about* Johnson. It was spoken by someone who did not know him well, but knew of him very well, William Gerard Hamilton. For me, it is Rhys Isaac's epitaph: " He has made a chasm, which not only nothing can fill up, but which nothing has a tendency to fill up. – Johnson is dead. – Let us go to the next best; – There is no nobody; – no man can be said to put you in mind of Johnson."

About the Author

GEORGE MORROW brings a lifetime of experience to bear on the characters of the people featured in this series. He has been a university instructor, lawyer, general counsel for a *Fortune* 100 company, the CEO of two major health care organizations and a management consultant. He received his academic training in textual analysis and literary theory from Rutgers and Brown Universities. He lives in Williamsburg with his wife, Joan, and two in-your-face Siamese cats, Pete and Pris.

WILLIAMSBURG IN CHARACTER

A Cock and Bull for Kitty
Lord Dunmore and the Affair that Ruined
the British Cause in Virginia

The Greatest Lawyer That Ever Lived
Patrick Henry at the Bar of History

The Day They Buried Great Britain
Francis Fauquier, Lord Botetourt and The Fate of Nations

Williamsburg at Dawn
The Duel That Touched Off A Revolution In Arthur Lee

Of Heretics, Traitors and True Believers
The War for the Soul of Williamsburg

George Washington and the Immortal Moment
Yorktown, 1781

Forthcoming

"War!"